The Collapse of the Kyoto Protocol

and the Struggle to Slow Global Warming

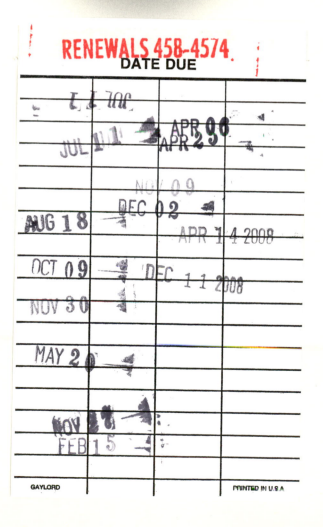

The Collapse of the Kyoto Protocol

and the Struggle to Slow Global Warming

With a new afterword by the author

DAVID G. VICTOR

A Council on Foreign Relations Book

PRINCETON UNIVERSITY PRESS
PRINCETON AND OXFORD

Copyright © 2001 by David G. Victor
Published by Princeton University Press, 41 William Street, Princeton, New Jersey 08540
In the United Kingdom: Princeton University Press, 3 Market Place, Woodstock, Oxfordshire OX20 1SY
All Rights Reserved

Sixth printing, and first paperback printing, with a new afterword and an updated preface, 2004
Paperback ISBN 0-691-12026-9

The Library of Congress has cataloged the cloth edition of this book as follows
Victor, David G.
The collapse of the Kyoto Protocol and the struggle to slow global warming / David G. Victor.
p. cm.
Includes bibliographical references and index.
ISBN 0-691-08870-5 (acid-free paper)
1. Global warming—Government policy. 2. Greenhouse gas mitigation— Government policy. 3. United Nations Framework Convention on Climate Change (1992). Protocols, etc., 1997 Dec. 11. I. Title.
QC981.8.G56 V53 2001   363.738'7456—dc21   00-051633

British Library Cataloging-in-Publication Data is available

This book has been composed in Berkeley

Printed on acid-free paper. ∞

pup.princeton.edu

Printed in the United States of America

7 9 10 8 6

Contents

Preface

The litany of global warming hazards is now familiar. Changing temperatures and rainfall may harm agriculture and stress natural ecosystems. Rising sea levels and severe storms may erode and inundate coastal zones. Especially worrisome is mounting evidence that nasty surprises, such as an abrupt shift in climate, become more likely as carbon dioxide and other "greenhouse gases" accumulate in the atmosphere. (The appendix to this book gives a brief survey of the science.) Although uncertainties are still pervasive, the dangers of greenhouse gases are not being ignored. Global warming is hardly the only environmental hazard, but in many countries it is rising high as a policy priority.

With a growing consensus for action, the world now faces the challenge of designing an effective policy response. International cooperation will be required because greenhouse gases are long-lived in the atmosphere—emissions from every country spread worldwide to create a truly global problem. Cooperation is also required because controlling emissions may be costly. Most of these emissions are the by-product of burning the fossil fuels that power modern industrial economies. Few nations or firms will do much to control emissions unless they are sure that their competitors will bear similar costs.[1] Fifteen years ago, the central challenge for global warming policy was simply to make industrial managers, government officials, and the public aware of the dangers. Today, awareness abounds and the main impediment to action is the lack of a viable architecture for international cooperation.

For more than a decade, governments have been building a framework for action. In 1992 at the "Earth Summit" in Rio, diplomats adopted the Framework Convention on Climate Change. That convention created systems for reporting data on emissions of greenhouse gases and other essential functions; it deferred agreement on the thornier problem of how actually to limit emissions of greenhouse gases. Five years later, diplomats completed the framework by adopting the "Kyoto Protocol," which sets targets and timetables for 38 nations to control emissions of greenhouse gases. For example, on average during the years 2008–2012, emissions from the countries in the European Union must be 8% below the 1990 level. Japan's required cut is 6%, while the United States committed to reduce its emissions 7%.

In the fall of 2000, when I finished this book, diplomats were trying to work out accounting rules and other crucial issues that they left vague in Kyoto. After they reached agreement on these final items, legislatures in the industrialized countries were expected to decide whether to ratify and implement the commitments they made in Kyoto. In setting the scene for this book, I argued that time had already run out. In the United States, especially, emissions had risen sharply since the early 1990s. Turning that economy around to meet the Kyoto limits would require a costly crash program. Even in Europe, where policy makers profess a much greater willingness to pay for emission controls, most countries were not on track to comply with the Kyoto limits.[2] What will governments do as these realities sink in?

This book explores the impending crisis. A new afterword comments on events from fall 2000 and January 2004, including the decision by the U.S. government to withdraw from Kyoto. My argument is that the gap between actual emissions and the Kyoto targets is not merely the result of giddy ambition that led governments to promise more than they could deliver during the early morning hours when they clinched their deal in Kyoto. Rather, the gaps are fundamental flaws in a regulatory system improvidently based on setting targets and timetables for controlling emissions of greenhouse gases.

Emissions vary with economic growth and technological change, neither of which can be planned by governments according to exacting targets. Since governments cannot plan future emission levels, they cannot be sure that they will comply with particular emission targets, such as those in the Kyoto Protocol. The proposed solution to this problem is "emission trading," which allows governments (and firms) to trade emission credits and debits. A nation in surplus can sell to another in deficit, allowing both to comply while costing society less than if each were forced to implement emission controls entirely on its own. Without emission trading, deficit nations such as the United States never would have agreed to stringent emission targets in Kyoto. Trading is the linchpin for the Kyoto framework.

However, the problem with trading is that it requires allocating permits that are worth hundreds of billions of dollars. In the past, countries have been able to allocate and launch trading systems within their own borders. For example, the United States has created a countrywide emission trading system for sulfur dioxide, a key precursor to acid rain. In Europe, governments have auctioned tens of billions of dollars of licenses for the third generation of mobile telephones (the so-called "3G auctions" or "spectrum auctions"). However, success in these limited domestic experiments offers little assurance that international permit trading will work. Trading of carbon permits across borders rests on international law, which is a weak force. Nations can withdraw if their allocation proves inconvenient, and there are few strong penalties available under international law that can keep them from defecting. Yet the integrity of an emission trading system requires the impossible: that major players not withdraw.

The impossibility of solving the allocation problem is moving to center stage as diplomats attempt to expand the Kyoto framework to include developing countries. Emissions from the developing world are rising rapidly and, within the next three decades, are likely to exceed those from the industrialized nations.[3] Yet developing countries are currently exempt from Kyoto's limits. The interests of the industrialized and developing worlds do not overlap, which seriously undermines the hope for achieving an acceptable and stable allocation. Industrialized nations want to allocate emission permits according to the status quo—that is, large allocations for today's big emitters. Developing countries want to overturn the status quo. Deal-makers imagine a grand bargain that could balance these conflicting interests, but I argue that no deal is durable. The grand bargainers might reach a pact—just as the diplomats in Kyoto finally got to agreement— but changing circumstances will aggrieve some. As the aggrieved and inconvenienced exit, the trading system will unravel.

Kyoto's troubles are the consequence of a public policy process that has been astonishingly uncritical about how best to manage global environmental problems. That process has manufactured a conventional wisdom that the only way to control pollution is to set inviolable targets and timetables for controlling emissions. That wisdom was locked into place with the success of the 1987 "Montreal Protocol on Substances that Deplete the Ozone Layer," which set targets and timetables for consumption of chlorofluorocarbons and other chemicals that thin the ozone layer. Few observers have given much attention to whether the Montreal precedent is appropriate for application to other global environmental problems; I will show that global warming is quite different and demands a very different solution. Ironically, one of the most important innovations in the Montreal Protocol is the inclusion of an "escape clause" that kicks in when controlling emissions becomes too costly. That precedent is extremely important for application to the global warming problem. One of the central reasons that governments are wary of implementing strict limits on greenhouse gases is the possibility that those limits will be much more costly than they had anticipated. Yet the "escape clause" innovation is the most commonly ignored lesson from the Montreal Protocol experience, and discussion of adding an escape clause to the Kyoto Protocol has triggered vehement opposition.

Emission trading is also the result of uncritical thinking about what works in international politics. Once governments had focused on setting targets and timetables for greenhouse gases it was merely a small step to imagine trading of those allocated targets. Again, diplomats had a successful precedent in mind— the U.S. system for trading sulfur dioxide credits—but gave too little attention to whether the precedent was applicable to the global warming problems.

While I argue that the core of the Kyoto architecture is flawed, not every element is wrongheaded. Among the important contributions of the Kyoto process have been the continued efforts to get countries to report useful data on their emissions of greenhouse gases and policies for controlling those emissions. The 1992 Framework Convention laid the foundation for that data collecting and analytical effort, and the Kyoto Protocol helped to sustain the momentum. The book also argues that Kyoto's Clean Development Mechanism (CDM) offered a way to engage developing countries in a global effort to build cleaner and more efficient energy systems. I argued that the CDM, although still ill defined in 2000, was important because it provides a basis for channeling market forces towards sensible projects in developing countries, rather than requiring a heavy-handed central public fund to make such investments. The afterword questions that conclusion in light of the poor progress with the CDM in recent years. Even as I question most of the Kyoto foundation, I am mindful that a key challenge is to sustain the positive elements of the Kyoto framework even as the rest of the system runs aground. Equally taxing will be to lock in progress on these important elements so that the successor to Kyoto need not start at zero.

The interest of this book for the growing community of policy makers engaged with the global warming issue should be obvious. Scholars, also, will find that I engage topics at the frontiers of their research. Atmospheric scientists, biologists, and foresters will find here the latest results from efforts to measure the fluxes of greenhouse gases applied to the problem of whether it is possible to monitor and verify compliance with the Kyoto Protocol (it isn't).[4] Economists and political scientists will recognize the tools of game theory and the logic of collective action applied to the thorny problem of how nations might allocate valuable emission permits.[5] Economists will also find reflected in these pages the important debate over whether "price" or "quantity" measures are the best way to regulate pollution.[6]

Fundamental to this book is the relationship between property rights and institutions, a central topic in economics and political science.[7] Launching an emission trading system requires creating a new form of property right—the right to emit greenhouse gases—and institutions to monitor, enforce, and secure those new property rights. I argue that the Kyoto Protocol fails principally because international law is a poor mechanism for securing property rights. This problem multiplies when the trading of these property rights must include the participation of countries that do not have strong and impartial national legal institutions, which is the case in most of the former Soviet Union and most developing countries.[8] Yet these "illiberal" nations are exactly the ones whose inclusion is critical for the main theoretical benefits of emission trading to be realized because they offer the lowest cost opportunities for emission control. Under international law, I argue, it is not possible to create the institutional conditions that are necessary for an international tradable emission permit system to operate effectively.

Kyoto's troubles indicate the need for clear thinking about the effectiveness of international treaties as devices for regulating behavior. The limited influence of international law requires careful design—to make the most of the levers that international law does offer. That topic is the subject of research on the process of "legalization" in international affairs, which is the focus of a fruitful collaboration between political scientists and international lawyers.[9] Although these debates from many different intellectual disciplines suffuse the analysis in this book, I have tried to keep the discussion jargon-free, brief, and focused on essentials. In that spirit, I have pushed important details and technical diversions into the many notes.

This book is one result of a research project, funded by the Energy Foundation and the Council on Foreign Relations, to investigate the role of "technology policy" as part of a strategy for managing the threats of global warming. My purpose was to examine how policy could help slow global warming by promoting innovation and the diffusion of new technologies. As I scrutinized whether and how technology policies might be effective, it became clear that the international framework for regulating emissions of greenhouse gases was a critical factor, and the Kyoto framework was deeply flawed—hence this book. Rod Nichols of the New York Academy of Sciences brilliantly chaired the project meetings and teased conclusions from our deliberations and my drafts that I never could have assembled alone. In addition to the Energy Foundation and Rod, I thank Les Gelb, Larry Korb, the Robert Wood Johnson 1962 Charitable Trust, and the John D. and Catherine T. MacArthur Foundation for their support of my tenure at the Council. Since leaving the Council as a full-time Fellow I have continued to work on climate policy at Stanford University with the Program on Energy and Sustainable Development, where I thank our core sponsors: the Electric Power Research Institute and BP.

I thank Bob Hahn and Jake Jacoby for detailed reviews of earlier drafts of the complete manuscript. Hadi Dowlatabadi, Dan Esty, Michael Grubb, Tom Heller, Marc Levy, Granger Morgan, Kal Raustiala, Rich Richels, Steve Schneider, Eugene Skolnikoff, Chris Stone, and several anonymous reviewers also provided critical reviews that spotted flaws in the argument and revealed new sources of information. While working on similar issues in international environmental regulation I have learned much from Jesse Ausubel, Abe Chayes, Arnulf Grübler, Tom Heller, Bob Keohane, Gordon MacDonald, Nebojša Nakićenović, Bill Nordhaus, Sten Nilsson, Ken Oye, Peter Sand, and Tom Schelling. This book, I hope, not only delivers a policy analysis on a particular topic—the troubled road from Kyoto—but also demonstrates why interdisciplinary research is worth the effort. Not one of the central issues in this book can be analyzed solely with the toolbox of a single discipline. I am grateful to have colleagues with such wide-ranging interests and training.

At Princeton University Press, Richard Baggaley has not only sharpened my writing but also generated contagious enthusiasm for the manuscript that has carried the production process at amazing speed. Although I address timeless issues of international cooperation and law, Richard has been mindful of the need for speed to ensure that this book is on hand as nations confront the crisis caused by their inability to ratify the Kyoto Protocol. At Princeton, I thank Ellen Foos for overseeing production and Jennifer Slater for scrutinizing every word and phrase; thanks, also, to Carolyn Hollis for overseeing the reissue of this book in 2004. Rebecca Weiner at the Council helped me edit several drafts of the manuscript; her careful eye is especially evident in chapter 1, which encapsulates the entire book's argument and is written with the thoughtful nonexpert in mind. Thanks also to Rebecca, Nora Kahn, and Henry Wong for able research assistance. My wife, Nadejda, not only wisely bolted me to our basement computer until the job was done, but also prepared all the statistics presented in this study and drafted the figures in chapters 1 and 2. A lucky man I am.

New York, NY
November, 2000
and
Palo Alto, CA
January, 2004

The Collapse of the Kyoto Protocol

and the Struggle to Slow Global Warming

Crisis and Opportunity

Worldwide, legislatures are beginning the long process of deciding whether to ratify and implement the December 1997 "Kyoto Protocol." Widely hailed as a first serious step towards slowing greenhouse warming, the protocol requires each industrialized nation to cap its emissions at specific target levels. Those targets apply to the "budget period" of 2008–2012, and the protocol also envisions that nations will agree on caps for future budget periods. Although public pressure to do something about global warming is growing, legislators will weigh the cost of compliance before they ratify the Kyoto deal. One factor will loom large in the debate: whether governments will be able to buy and sell emission credits—a scheme known as emission trading.

Without emission trading, nations would be required to meet their Kyoto obligations entirely within their borders. In the United States, for example, compliance would require a Herculean effort. By the end of 1999, U.S. emissions had risen about 12% above 1990 levels and were on track to rise another 10% by 2008.[1] Yet the Kyoto Protocol requires a 7% cut *below* 1990 levels—in total, about a 30% cut. Turning the economy around to meet the Kyoto target could cost over $1000 per household per year, which is similar to the annual spending on all federal clean air and water programs combined.[2] The cost would be high because most emissions of greenhouse gases come from burning fossil fuels for energy, and the economic lifetime of energy equipment like power plants, buildings, and automobiles is long (two decades or more). Compliance with a sharp 30% cut would force the premature disposal of some of the "capital stock" of energy equipment and retard significant parts of the U.S. economy. Electric power generation is especially vulnerable. About half of U.S. electric power is supplied by coal, which is the most greenhouse gas intensive of all fossil fuels. The time to implement easy changes has already passed. About four-fifths of the U.S. generating capacity that will electrify 2010 will already have been built by the end of the year 2000.

With trading, however, nations could lower the cost of capping emissions. For example, a trading system could allow U.S. firms to purchase emission credits overseas, which might be much cheaper than making all the needed emission controls at home. The Kyoto Protocol envisions three interrelated trading systems. One, known formally as emission trading, would allow an industrialized country to increase its emission cap by purchasing part of another industrialized nation's Kyoto allocation. A second system, known as joint implementation (JI), would allow industrialized countries to earn credits when they jointly implement specific projects that reduce emissions. A third System, known as the Clean Development Mechanism (CDM), allows industrialized nations to earn credits for projects implemented within developing nations.[3]

Together, these three systems—emission trading, JI, and the CDM—could constitute a full-blown emission trading system that would allow firms to shop the world for the least costly ways to reduce emissions. Nations would have the ultimate responsibility for complying with treaties under international law, and thus national governments would bear the ultimate responsibility for ensuring that the trading books balance. In practice, however, firms and individuals would probably do most of the trading. The economic appeal of trading is substantial. In the United States, full-blown trading could lower the annual costs by a factor of ten—to a more palatable $100 per American household.[4]

As figure 1.1 illustrates, nearly all other advanced industrialized countries are in a similar situation. In Japan, emissions have risen more slowly than in the United States because Japanese economic performance for the last decade has been dismal. Nonetheless, Japan is not on track to comply with its Kyoto target (6% cut below 1990 levels) unless it can purchase credits overseas.

In Europe, emissions have actually declined slightly since 1990. Economic collapse and modernization in eastern Germany explain most of the reduction; in addition, energy market reforms in the United Kingdom have caused a shift from carbon-intensive coal towards carbon-light natural gas and zero-carbon nuclear power. Nonetheless, these events have not put the 15 countries of the European Union on track to comply with their Kyoto commitment to cut emissions 8% below the 1990 level during 2008–2012.[5] That is why, after vigorously decrying emission trading as an American ruse to avoid any serious cuts in greenhouse gas emissions, the European Union (EU) is now developing a plan to implement a credit trading system that would enable it to meet some of its Kyoto obligation by purchasing emission credits overseas.[6]

After long opposing trading as a loophole that would let industrialized countries avoid their duty to slow global warming, a growing number of developing countries are also beginning to embrace trading cautiously. Exempt from Kyoto's regulatory obligations, developing nations have been wary of participating in international efforts to slow global warming because they fear that they, too, will be expected to implement costly controls on emissions of greenhouse gases in the future. Through the CDM,

5

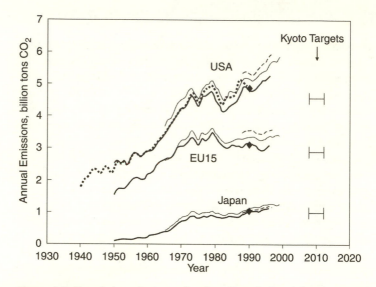

FIGURE 1.1: Trends in emissions of carbon dioxide (CO_2) from combustion of fossil fuels for the United States, European Union (EU15), and Japan. Although several gases are responsible for global warming, CO_2 from fossil fuels is the most important and best documented. Shown are CO_2 emissions calculated from four semi-independent data sets for consumption of fossil fuels: (a) solid heavy lines, Oak Ridge National Laboratory (Marland et al., 1993; updated at www.cdiac.ornl.gov); (b) light dashed lines, EIA (1999); (c) solid light lines, BP Amoco (2000); and (d) dashed heavy lines, the IIASA/WEC data sets, which are based on International Energy Agency energy balance statistics and reported by Nakićenović et al. (1998). The estimates shown for CO_2 are computed using common heating values and carbon emission coefficients, and thus the variance in the emissions is a consequence of differences in the underlying data for combustion of fossil fuels. Also shown (♦) are data officially reported for the base year (1990) in the "national communications" by the European Union, Japan, and the United States to the Framework Convention on Climate Change. Bars during 2008–2012 illustrate the Kyoto targets, which are calculated from the reported base year statistics. Note that, although the figure shows only CO_2 from fossil fuels, the Kyoto Protocol includes six gases—these other gases account for much smaller shares of total global warming, and reliable time series for these data are not available. The figure also omits "sinks" of CO_2 due to growing forests and changes in land use, since governments have not agreed on accounting rules for including these sinks.

however, they could attract new investment into projects that limit emissions of greenhouse gases, stem other environmental problems such as urban smog associated with dirty fossil fuels, and modernize their energy systems.[7]

Thus a consensus is emerging worldwide that trading is the key to realizing the Kyoto Protocol. For the western industrialized nations, emission trading makes the protocol's targets and timetables appear cost effective and feasible. For developing countries, full-blown emission trading offers the best chance to benefit from a worldwide effort to slow global warming. Trading is the keystone of the architecture adopted in Kyoto.

This monograph explores the political, economic, and technical issues that policy makers must address prior to creating a complete emission trading system. It argues that, when viewed in totality, the hurdles to be cleared are so daunting that a sensible emission trading system is infeasible in the foreseeable future. It also argues that the diplomats who crafted the Kyoto Protocol have painted themselves into a corner. In Kyoto they achieved agreement by setting emission targets that would be politically impossible to implement without an emission trading system; yet they deferred discussion of all the details about how the system would operate. During their first high-level meeting after Kyoto—held in November 1998 in Buenos Aires—diplomats set a hopelessly optimistic timetable for resolving by late 2000 all 152 "elements" left outstanding in Kyoto.[8] Individually, nearly every element—such as "compliance," "reporting," and "independent certification and verification"—is difficult to settle; together, the task is impossible. A longer timetable would make it easier to complete the job, but it would also shorten the time left between completion of the emission trading framework and the date when emission targets must be met.

With the clock ticking towards 2008, and the fate of the Kyoto Protocol hanging in the balance, what should be done? Should political leaders soldier on, ratify the protocol, and hope for the best? Should they retain the targets and trading architecture that

7

they created in Kyoto but stretch out the timetables to make it easier to comply? Or should they use Kyoto's troubles as an opportunity to construct a different framework for slowing global warming?

Most governments plan to soldier on, but that option has the least to recommend it because it forces countries to select among three dead ends. First, diplomats might make it easier to comply with the Kyoto caps on emissions by creating convenient accounting systems. Notably, the protocol includes language that allows countries to take credit for "sinks" that remove CO_2, the most important greenhouse gas, from the atmosphere. When plants grow they accumulate carbon in their trunks, stems, roots, and leaves—as well as in surrounding soils. Agricultural soils are important sinks. In the United States, for example, starting in about 1910—when tractors made it easier for farmers to plow deeper—intensive tilling has reduced the carbon content of soils. Since the 1950s, farmers have been shifting to "no till" techniques that have helped slow soil erosion while also fortuitously increasing the carbon content of soils. Forests are especially large sinks—forests are growing larger and denser in all the advanced industrialized countries, in part because intensive farming is reducing the need for cropland and some of the abandoned land reverts to forest.[9]

Luck and clever accounting could deliver large credits for these sinks. One data set suggests that the United States could offset about 14% of its current emissions if it were awarded full credit for "land-use change and forestry"—a significant down payment that could amount to nearly half of the required reduction during 2008–2012.[10] The more credit awarded for CO_2 that plants and trees are already absorbing, the easier it is for nations to comply with the Kyoto Protocol targets without actually changing behavior.

But this strategy founders on the lack of widely accepted definitions, methods, and data for counting sinks.[11] Even if nations could agree on the necessary procedures, there would still be enormous potential for cooking the books—only a monitoring program larger and more intrusive than anything ever attempted under international law could settle the inevitable disputes. Moreover, the carbon content of forests and soils varies naturally—decades of monitoring would be needed to be certain that a "sink" was not merely transient and deserved full credit.[12] Yet the commitment periods under international law are typically much shorter, such as the five-year "budget period" of the Kyoto Protocol.

A second dead end is for nations in deficit to earn credits overseas through the CDM. Diplomats still have not been able to agree on the rules that would govern the CDM system, and thus investors are still not sure whether and how they could earn credits through these mechanisms. Yet years of preparation, testing, and learning will be required to build a pipeline of sensible projects. Time has run out for firms and governments to earn large quantities of credits by investing in emission-reducing projects under the CDM.

Emission trading is a third way to ease compliance, but it also leads to a dead end. Governments must solve considerable technical problems that confound trading—which I discuss in the following chapters. But even if they succeed, this scenario poses a significant political problem. Russia and Ukraine are by far the cheapest sources of emission credits—not because the Russians and Ukrainians have had an epiphany about the risks of global warming but rather because their savvy negotiators got an emission target in Kyoto that far exceeds the likely level of emissions. Russia and Ukraine agreed in Kyoto to freeze emissions at 1990 levels, but the collapse of the post-Soviet economy in the early 1990s means that their emissions are already far below that target and unlikely to recover fully by 2008. Selling the windfall to nations in emissions deficit—notably the United States—could earn Russia and Ukraine perhaps $100 billion.[13] (About four-fifths of that windfall would flow to Russia.) Since the windfall is free—completely an artifact of the luck and skill of the diplo-

9

mats in Kyoto rather than the result of any effort to control emissions—these extra credits would squeeze out bona fide efforts to control emissions. That buys paper compliance but no reduction in global warming. No Western legislature will ratify a deal that merely enriches Russia and Ukraine while doing nothing to control emissions and slow global warming.

Nonetheless, the pressure to soldier on and preserve the Kyoto framework is strong. Bureaucratic inertia favors such muddling, since change is threatening to the international and national institutions that are now engaged full time in working on the Kyoto issue. Change would also endanger other cars that have attached themselves to the Kyoto train—for example, energy ministries in many countries have used the Kyoto framework as impetus for rekindling interest in energy policy. Intellectual inertia also favors keeping the Kyoto framework intact—since 1991, remarkably few analysts have examined any alternatives to the "cap and trade" architecture that was codified in the Kyoto Protocol.

These reasons explain why governments are now following the worst strategy—implementing all three of the Kyoto-saving devices simultaneously. Through clever "sink" accounting they hope to make the targets less onerous. Through JI and especially the CDM they hope to earn credits overseas. And through emission trading they aim to reduce the cost of full compliance. But, as we will see, creating an emission trading system requires creating emission permits worth hundreds of billions of dollars. Including difficult-to-measure sinks will undermine confidence in the value of those emission permits and give governments strong financial incentive to cook the books. Including the CDM offers a way to earn credits, but putting the CDM into practice will prove to be very slow and inefficient.

Governments cannot solve these problems unless they reopen the protocol—to tighten the targets for Russia and the other transition countries and to distinguish between fluxes of greenhouse gases that can be monitored accurately and those that are harder to count (notably, CO_2 sinks). Diplomats are loathe to do that; they know that agreement in Kyoto was possible only because negotiators left in shadow the rules that would govern their imaginary emission trading system. Attempts to clarify and fix these rules will provoke deep disagreements and accelerate Kyoto's collapse.

Unable to keep the Kyoto deal as written, diplomats will thus try the next most attractive option: preserving the framework but stretching out the timetables to make compliance easier. That option merely delays the day of reckoning. The Kyoto framework is based on a fundamentally wrong assumption that it is best to slow global warming by setting strict targets and timetables for regulating the *quantity* of greenhouse gases emitted.

Regulating emission quantities is problematic because emissions are determined by factors such as technological change and economic growth that policy makers are unable to control or anticipate perfectly. If governments had control over all the factors that affect emissions then they could calibrate national behavior perfectly and comply with sensible targets, but in democratic market-based countries public administrators are neither omniscient nor omnipotent. The same logic obliges countries to adopt national trading systems that link with the international system.[14] Because nations cannot be sure of their future emission levels, the only cost-effective way to balance the books is to allow international emission trading. Emission targets beget trading. Imposing strict limits on emission quantities requires a system for trading credits and debits.

The problem with trading is that it requires solving a nearly impossible problem before trading can begin: governments must allocate the emission permits. Because no nation knows its future level of emissions or the cost of controlling emissions, no nation will know how many permits it will need. Diplomats, properly trained to protect national interests, will seek allocations based on a worst-case perspective. They will imagine scenarios where their nation's future emissions and costs of control are much higher than expected. Each will demand a large share

11

of the total number of permits and feel harmed by the share awarded to other countries. The difficulty of allocating benefits and burdens is hardly new to international politics; allocation will confound any collective effort to slow global warming. But emission trading makes solving the allocation problem much harder—chapter 2 explores the three reasons why.

First, emission trading magnifies the stakes. Emission permits are semipermanent property rights. In any well-functioning market, property rights are much more valuable than the annual flow of payments based on those assets. For example, it costs more to buy a house than to rent it for a year. High stakes will make diplomats wary, which will cause them to be especially cautious in the first allocation because that will set the framework for subsequent adjustments and reallocations. That is why diplomats spent years in the Law of the Sea negotiations haggling over how to allocate deep seabed mining rights even though deep seabed mining was largely untested and mining rights had only hypothetical future value. By comparison, imagine how difficult it will be to allocate greenhouse gas emission permits of immediate value that are certain to be worth hundreds of billions of dollars.

Second, a key obstacle is gaining the consent of firms and governments that must pay the cost of acquiring permits. In earlier trading systems—such as the U.S. system for controlling acid rain, or New Zealand's system for tradable fishing quotas —policy makers eased this problem by "grandfathering" permits. They blunted political opposition by giving valuable property rights to the same entities that they most expected to oppose the scheme. But this strategy does not work for an international emission trading system. The trading system must be able to accommodate new entrants—developing countries—who will demand allocations that are quite different from the status quo. Emissions from developing countries are rising much more rapidly than those from the industrialized world, and governments in the developing world think that their future economic growth demands much higher emissions still. For the developing countries, grandfathering is unacceptable.

Third, the economic efficiency of trading depends on the integrity of the emission permits, which are a form of property right. Yet it is extremely difficult to secure property rights under international law. To date, all significant experience with emission trading is within nations where the state is strong and able to impose the rule of law that is necessary to secure property rights. In contrast, international law has no central authority that can compel countries to remain part of a treaty. The high value of emission permits increases the likelihood that countries will attempt to defect, and the need for security of property rights increases the consequences of defection.

The typical pattern of international diplomacy magnifies the difficulty. Normally, diplomats craft international treaties and then must wait several years as their countries ratify the deal and bring it into legal force. Costly treaties that involve many countries typically require the longest time to ratify. That is problematic because the allocation is based on information about future emission levels and abatement costs that is imperfect. As time elapses, those factors also change; as the date for starting the system approaches, countries whose emissions are far above their allocation will seek reallocation or withdraw from the treaty. But new allocations will affect the costs for all others and unravel the agreement. Recent trends illustrate the problem. Projections of U.S. emissions made since the 1997 Kyoto conference have been markedly higher than the earlier projections that formed a basis for negotiations in Kyoto. The U.S. economy has been more robust than analysts expected on Kyoto's eve. In contrast, emissions from Russia and Ukraine remain lower than most experts anticipated, and thus their windfall allocation of emission permits is even larger.

I call these three the "cold start" problems. Trading requires first the creation and allocation of property rights. However, the constant threat of defection makes it extraordinarily difficult to allocate and secure property rights. Yet secure property rights are the cornerstone of emission trading. Chapter 2 explores ways to solve the "cold start" problems, but I find no solution for the key problem: the weakness of international law.

Why did diplomats venture into this swamp by creating an architecture based on targets and timetables for emission quantities? At the time that diplomats were framing the Kyoto Protocol and its parent agreement—the 1992 Framework Convention on Climate Change—the working model for international environmental treaties was the 1987 Montreal Protocol on Substances that Deplete the Ozone Layer. The Montreal Protocol set targets and timetables for regulating consumption of ozone-depleting substances, and nearly all nations have since complied. The Montreal Protocol was widely seen as the most effective treaty in the history of international environmental diplomacy, and rightly so—it is why ozone-destroying substances such as chlorofluorocarbons are being phased out worldwide and why the thinning ozone layer is now poised to heal.

Barely a year after diplomats signed the Montreal Protocol they gathered again, in Toronto, for the first major international conference on political strategies for slowing global warming. The Toronto conference ended with the call for nations to cut CO_2 emissions 20% below 1990 levels by 2005. No major nation had a plan for how it would reach the Toronto target—and nearly all will fail to achieve that goal—but that did not slow subsequent efforts to set even more targets and timetables. In 1991, when negotiations on a formal global warming treaty began, many countries and pressure groups made the adoption of binding targets and timetables their central goal. They failed, and the 1992 Framework Convention on Climate Change included no clear targets and timetables. Advocates pushed the same agenda, with success, at the first meeting of the convention's supreme decision-making body—the Conference of the Parties (COP-1), held in Berlin in 1995. The result was the "Berlin Mandate," which gave the legal marching orders for the negotiating process that led to the 1997 Kyoto Protocol. The Berlin Mandate specifically required that the Kyoto Protocol should set "quantified limitation and reduction objectives within specified time frames." In plain language: the Kyoto Protocol should set targets and timetables for emission quantities.[15]

The architects of the Montreal Protocol never had to confront the central problems of trading. They established only an extremely limited emission trading system. The treaty expected that advanced industrialized nations would eliminate ozone-depleting substances on their own, rather than earning credits for overseas efforts. Initially, the goal was to cut consumption by half. With the ink on the Montreal agreement barely dry, incontrovertible evidence that these substances caused the ozone "hole" over Antarctica (and a lesser thinning of ozone worldwide) forced diplomats to tighten the goal to a complete phaseout of all major ozone-depleting substances. Compared with global warming, agreeing on the effort to control ozone-depleting substances was easier because the economic stakes were much lower. Producers and users of ozone-depleting substances soon found substitutes for nearly all applications of the most harmful compounds.

With the Montreal Protocol, diplomats matched the architecture of the treaty with the environmental ill they were trying to solve. Caps on emissions made sense because there was a widely agreed goal of avoiding a relatively clear and dangerous threshold. Scientists demonstrated that even tiny concentrations of chlorine and bromine in the stratosphere would trigger the ozone "hole." Once the advanced industrialized nations agreed that the "hole" must be healed it was clear that essentially all uses of ozone-depleting substances must be eliminated. And once elimination was the collective goal there could be no debate over allocation—each nation individually had to achieve a phaseout. They wrangled over the timing and over how to phase out some minor ozone-depleting substances, but the central goal forced focus. Developing countries were more skeptical and op-

15

posed costly requirements to eliminate ozone-depleting substances. These countries are concentrated nearer the tropics where ozone depletion is less severe, and their governments were under much less political pressure to act—development, rather than costly environmental controls with distant benefits, was their aspiration. Once the advanced industrialized nations created a fund to compensate developing countries for the extra cost of complying with the Montreal Protocol phaseout and threatened trade sanctions against any country that did not participate, the developing nations shifted. Today, almost all are on track to eliminate nearly all their consumption of ozone-depleting substances.

Finally, the architects of the Montreal Protocol paid close attention to technical feasibility and economic costs. They created an "escape clause" that allowed countries to exempt important uses of ozone-depleting substances from regulation, which countries have often invoked in cases where it has been too costly to find substitutes. (Regular technical reviews kept countries from abusing the escape clause.) This provision in the protocol made it easier to allocate strict emission targets because it allowed countries to avoid extremely onerous commitments. Political support for protecting the ozone layer would have suffered badly if asthmatics had been forced to abandon medicines in metered-dose inhalers (MDIs). MDIs account for a tiny fraction of ozone-depleting substances, but finding substitutes for their chlorofluorocarbon propellant has proved much trickier than for most other uses of ozone-depleting substances.[16]

The Montreal Protocol loomed large when diplomats sought to build a regulatory regime to slow global warming. But they gave inadequate attention to whether the right lessons had been learned from the Montreal Protocol experience, and to whether the lessons were relevant for the global warming problem. Global warming diplomats should have taken more seriously the problem of allocating emission permits, which did not confound the Montreal process as much as it will when hundreds of billions of dollars of tradable assets are at stake. And they should have paid closer attention to the obscure but vitally important escape provisions of the Montreal Protocol, which made it easier to contain compliance costs. As we will see, provisions that make it possible to contain costs also make it easier to allocate emission permits.

Assuming that, somehow, diplomats might solve the allocation problem, chapter 3 examines other functions that are also necessary for an effective emission trading system—in particular, monitoring of compliance and enforcement.

Kyoto's architects gave little attention to the crucial role of monitoring. The protocol's targets apply to a basket of six greenhouse gases—carbon dioxide, methane, nitrous oxide, and other gases. The problem is that it is difficult to monitor emissions of most of these gases because the activities that cause the emissions are not well understood. The exception is carbon dioxide emitted during combustion of fossil fuels—that flux is extremely well measured and (luckily) also accounts for most of the increase in greenhouse warming.

All schemes to slow global warming must contend with monitoring problems, but they pose special challenges for emission trading. If the fluxes of some gases can't be measured accurately then permits can't be assigned reliably. The security of the underlying property rights erodes, and with this the efficiency of the trading system declines. A simple and effective solution to this problem would involve restricting an emission trading system to fossil fuel emissions of carbon dioxide—at least initially, until the monitoring problems for the other gases are fixed. Diplomats have resisted that because they erroneously think that the only way to address the entire global warming problem and to build an emission trading system is to lump all the gases together into a single system.

Enforcement is a perennial problem of international law, but emission trading potentially offers an elegant solution. If buyers were held responsible for the integrity of the permits they own

17

then the market would price permits according to their origin and risk of default. Since most permits would be used in advanced industrialized nations, where the rule of law is strong and legal institutions are efficient, buyers would be held accountable through their national legal systems.

It is odd, then, that a consensus is developing in favor of "seller liability," which would hold Russia, Ukraine, and other major sellers liable for their own compliance—letting buyers off the hook the moment after the permit changes hands. This strange scheme would give sellers a strong incentive to flood the market with bogus permits, knowing that international institutions rarely muster the swift and painful enforcement that would be needed to avert the practice. Worse, if a penalty were imminent the seller could withdraw from the Protocol, pocketing the sale proceeds and leaving the bogus permits in circulation. A strong compliance mechanism could avert that outcome, but there is no precedent for such a mechanism in international environmental law. Moreover, the Kyoto Protocol prohibits the parties from adopting a compliance mechanism that imposes "binding consequences" unless governments formally amend the Protocol. Because amending the Protocol would reopen and unravel the Kyoto deal, diplomats have been doubly wary of crafting a compliance mechanism that is adequate to the task. Seller liability is like an autoimmune disorder; it creates incentives that tempt parties to undermine the trading system, and once overselling begins the unraveling accelerates.

Should diplomats redouble their efforts to find solutions to trading troubles, or are better alternatives available? Chapter 4 explores these questions by comparing four major options for the architecture of a global warming treaty. It argues that the Kyoto approach of capping emissions at particular quantities makes sense only if the objective of international efforts to slow global warming is to avert a catastrophe that would be triggered by a certain accumulation of emissions in the atmosphere. Governments would identify the dangerous threshold, cap emissions below the level, and allow trading so that firms could meet the cap at the lowest cost. Diplomats envisioned exactly this approach when they created the Framework Convention on Climate Change. In Article 2 they defined the central objective of international cooperation on climate change as to stabilize concentrations of greenhouse gases "at a level that would prevent dangerous anthropogenic interference with the climate system." The approach appears to be elegant and sensible but is unworkable. It is not (yet) possible to identify particular thresholds that would trigger horrible climate changes. Worse, if governments set short-term emission caps too tightly they may force their economies to bear extremely high costs of cutting emissions more rapidly than can be achieved with the orderly turnover of the capital stock.

In theory, a better approach would focus on coordinating emission taxes. Governments would implement taxes that begin at a low level and rise over time. An international agreement would set the tax levels and a schedule for adjusting them. By controlling the price of emissions, this approach makes it easier for firms to anticipate the cost of emission controls and to plan long-term investments. It does not require that diplomats invent a hypothetical cap on the exact quantity of emissions. Because it makes it easier to contain costs, a tax system is economically more intelligent than a cap and trade system.[17] Moreover, the tax approach may make it easier for governments to solve the thorny allocation problem because it does not require allocating and securing property rights in the form of emission permits. In practice, however, a tax system is extremely difficult to monitor and enforce. Governments would implement greenhouse gas taxes on top of existing distortions in their tax systems, making it hard to measure the practical effect of the new taxes. In principle, they could create an international regulatory body that would conduct inspections and run economic models to assess tax policy; in practice, such an institution would be much more intrusive and powerful than most governments are likely to tolerate.

19

Chapter 4 concludes that the best architecture for a global warming treaty is a hybrid of the trading and tax systems. Governments would set targets for emission quantities as well as targets for emission prices. Having limited quantities, governments would create an emission trading system. Unlike a textbook emission trading system, however, governments would also commit to selling additional permits at the target price. The cost of permits would therefore never rise above the target price.[18]

In contrast with a textbook emission trading system, the hybrid approach would make it much easier for governments to anticipate the cost of compliance. The hybrid system eliminates the possibility that compliance costs would be much higher than expected. By containing costs, the hybrid architecture greatly eases the "cold start" problem of emission trading. In a textbook emission trading system, governments will be risk averse because they fear the possibility that emissions will be higher, and abatement more costly, than expected. The hybrid system eliminates this worst-case scenario and makes it easier to agree on an initial allocation of emission permits.

Greater control over costs would also make it easier for governments to limit the financial flows that could occur when the system is switched on. If governments are more confident about the cost of abatement it will be easier for them to allocate permits according to marginal cost. Financial flows—such as the windfalls that would flow to Russia and Ukraine under the Kyoto scheme—arise when marginal costs differ markedly. When costs are contained it will be politically easier for governments to resist demands for extra headroom.

In a textbook emission trading system the number of permits remains fixed, and the demand for permits governs the price. In a textbook tax system the tax level governs the price, and the quantity of emissions varies. In a hybrid system both quantities and prices can vary. Demand for permits controls the price up to the target price; above that level, governments print new permits and the price is constant.

The target price would perform a function similar to the "escape clause" in the Montreal Protocol—if compliance proved too onerous the regulatory system would shift the goalposts to a tolerable position. In contrast, without an "escape clause" governments could be forced to bear unplanned burdens or, more likely, to tear down the goalposts by withdrawing from the treaty.

A hybrid approach would also be much easier to monitor and enforce. Unlike an emission tax, it would not require governments to implement extra taxes on top of existing distortions in their tax systems. Rather, the market would govern the price of emission permits, making it easy to determine whether governments are selling additional permits at the agreed price level. Requirements to mark the origin of every permit—as in government debt markets today—would make it easy to spot a government that floods the market with below-cost permits. As with a textbook emission trading system, buyer liability would be the best scheme for enforcement.[19]

Although this monograph is about the architecture for international agreements for controlling emissions, mainly emissions of carbon dioxide, I am mindful of the other dimensions to the global warming problem. In addition to whatever system is adopted for limiting emissions of carbon dioxide, four other types of policy are needed. First, governments must invest in knowledge. There is widespread agreement on the need to fund research and monitoring on the global warming problem itself. Also necessary are investments in long-term basic research in fields that are likely to make it easier to invent and apply new emission control technologies—physics, material sciences, nuclear engineering, and the like. Because basic knowledge is a public good—easily transmitted and difficult to appropriate— even if governments agree to control emissions, proper investments in basic research will not automatically follow. There is mounting evidence that advanced industrialized countries are already underinvesting in basic energy-related sciences.[20] Yet

21

over the last decade spending trends on such basic research in most advanced industrialized countries have been negative,[21] despite articulate plans for how government can help reverse this ebbing tide.[22] The challenges are large, especially as a great effort to increase spending should be part of an international knowledge strategy—because basic knowledge is an *international* public good—and not only set according to national priorities and institutions.[23]

Second, governments must also invest in adaptation. Many effects of global warming—such as flooding from storm surges and higher sea levels—are unavoidable. Societies must anticipate and prepare to adjust to those effects. Adaptation policies make sense even without the fear of global warming. Most of the anticipated effects of global warming on humans are already within the realm of humanity's experience with nature—even without global warming, buildings flood, crops wither, and nature dominates the outdoors. The same policies that soften the blows of nature also ease adaptation to the effects of global warming.

Third, governments should make some investment in "geoengineering"—the ability to make large-scale interventions in the climate system to slow or reverse climate change.[24] Mirrors in space, for example, could reflect sunlight and cool the planet—unfurled at the same pace that greenhouse gases accumulate they could keep Earth's thermostat level. Critics have rightly worried that geoengineering gone awry could do more harm than good. Technological interventions often have unanticipated consequences, and vigilance is needed.[25] But equally sobering is that greenhouse warming could trigger nasty surprises in the climate system, and if we detect one of those surprises then geoengineering will be the only option for quick intervention. It is not palatable, but advance preparation through research can reduce the dangers.

Fourth, governments need to clarify the objective of their efforts to control emissions of greenhouse gases. Goals are needed to focus the effort—even draft goals that will require revision but can focus debate during the interim. Yet the architects of the Kyoto system made two decisions that have deflated attention to proper goal setting. One decision derives from the conventional wisdom that treaties are the most effective instruments of international law. The consequence is that essentially all serious diplomatic discussions of goal setting have occurred within the context of negotiating two legally binding treaties—the Framework Convention on Climate Change and the Kyoto Protocol. Yet binding treaty negotiations are constantly shadowed by worries about compliance—a terrible atmosphere for debating uncertain and distant goals with uncertain economic consequences. More productive goal setting occurs in nonbinding frameworks where diplomats are less narrowly concerned with compliance and more likely to focus first on goals that make ecological and economic sense.

The other disservice of the Kyoto process was lumping all greenhouse gases into a single "basket" and treating them as freely interchangeable commodities. In reality, the gases have different lifetimes and merit distinct approaches. Methane is a strong greenhouse gas but lives only a relatively short time in the atmosphere (ten years). If our goal is to avoid climate changes in the next few decades then controlling methane is a quick way to get results,[26] but methane controls today are largely irrelevant for global warming problems that extend past 2020 or 2030. At the other extreme are sulfur hexafluoride (SF_6) and perfluorocarbons (PFCs). These greenhouse gases are thousands of times stronger in effect than CO_2 and linger in the atmosphere for thousands of years. Because of this long-term liability, and because firms can eliminate nearly all emissions of these gases at relatively low cost, governments should adopt policies to curtail these gases on a separate (and more stringent) timetable from the others.[27] Most climate policy is appropriately focused on CO_2, which causes most global warming that current and near future generations will experience, but it must not ignore the long-term liability of industrial society. The one-basket approach obscures these important distinctions, making it easier for most

23

policy makers to pretend that the time horizon of climatic effects does not matter.[28]

Chapter 5 recapitulates the message. When the Kyoto Protocol fails, policy makers must ensure that they and the public learn the right lessons. Analysts are pinning Kyoto's imminent demise on the wrong factors—on fleeting political will, on the expectation that Kyoto's costs far outweigh its environmental benefits, and on the fear that Kyoto will create strong and intrusive international institutions that will harm national democracies and freedoms.[29] This monograph argues that, while these factors are important, the demise of the Kyoto Protocol is largely the consequence of its very architecture.

The danger is not that the Kyoto Protocol will collapse. Rather, it is that governments will not reckon with Kyoto's real problems—that they will try to muddle through by stretching out the timetables rather than rethinking objectives and strategy. The governments that crafted and signed the Kyoto Protocol, and the nongovernmental organizations (NGOs) that have encouraged them, feel—like mother and child—that to walk away would mean betrayal. But separation is the first step to real action.

CHAPTER 2
Kyoto's Fantasyland: Allocating the Atmosphere

By far the most difficult problem for emission trading is distributing the permits. Nearly all studies on the economics of emission trading have treated the political problem of allocation as the proverbial economist's can opener. Assume an omnibus negotiation that distributes emission permits across 190 countries and several generations. Then wonder at the efficient market that can result. Is the assumption valid?

The standard critique of trading is that there exists no consensus on what formula can be used to govern the allocation of permits.[1] Emission trading enthusiasts—especially the Clinton Administration, which pushed hardest for emission trading in Kyoto—counter that the successful negotiation of the Kyoto Protocol is proof that permits can be allocated. They also claim that any collective agreement must allocate benefits and burdens—emission trading is no different; rather, the ability to compensate reluctant participants with excess permits might actually ease the problem of allocation. Moreover, enthusiasts argue that allocation problems have been solved in other emission trading systems, such as the successful U.S. program to trade emission rights for sulfur dioxide, the main precursor to acid rain.

On all three claims—the events in Kyoto, the similar allocation difficulties with nontrading mechanisms, and the relevance of domestic trading programs as precedents for international trading—the enthusiasts have focused on the wrong lessons.

The Kyoto Pact: Agreement by Avoidance

The Kyoto Protocol was negotiated in great haste, with most of the agreement assembled in just two months prior to the final negotiating session in December 1997. That compressed negotiating process gave almost no attention to how the commitments would be implemented, and thus negotiators essentially ignored the huge financial implications of the system they were creating. More than anything, negotiators from the advanced industrialized countries wanted a deal—any deal—that would give the impression that their governments were taking global warming seriously. They deferred final agreement on almost every issue that would determine the allocation of Kyoto's costs. They agreed in principle to create an emission trading system; yet the actual legal language in the Protocol does not require the creation of such a system. Diplomats from key countries—notably the United States—left Kyoto with the assumption that emission trading was integral to the pact; yet they deferred until later any effort to settle the rules that would govern that system. Speedy agreement in Kyoto was possible because a great veil of uncertainty put all the critical details in shadow.[2]

Thus the curious result: By setting emission targets, negotiators in effect allocated permits that are worth over $2 trillion (table 2.1). In principle, the parties did not actually create the permits because they deferred a decision on emission trading until later. Yet, in practice, few nations would be able to meet their strict Kyoto targets in a cost-effective manner unless they

TABLE 2.1
The Kyoto Allocation of Atmospheric Assets

ountry	1990 emissions (million tons of carbon dioxide)	Kyoto target ("assigned amount") (average % of 1990 levels 2008–2012)	Total asset value (billion U.S. dollars at $14 per ton of carbon dioxide)
ustralia	289	108	53
ustria	59	92	9
·lgium	113	92	18
ılgaria	97	92	15
anada	457	94	73
roatia	30	95	5
zech Republic	170	92	27
·nmark	52	92	8
·tonia	38	92	6
nland	54	92	8
·ance	367	92	58
·rmany	1012	92	159
reece	82	92	13
ıngary	84	94	13
·land	2	110	0.4
·land	31	92	5
ıly	429	92	67
pan	1173	94	188
.tvia	23	92	4
echtenstein	0.2	92	0.03
thuania	20	92	3
ıxembourg	11	92	2
onaco	0.1	92	0.01
·therlands	168	92	26
·w Zealand	26	100	4
·rway	36	101	6
·land	479	94	77
·rtugal	42	92	7
·mania	198	92	31
ıssia	2389	100	408
·vakia	58	92	9
·venia	30	92	5

TABLE 2.1
The Kyoto Allocation of Atmospheric Assets (*cont'd*)

Country	1990 emissions (million tons of carbon dioxide)	Kyoto target ("assigned amount") (average % of 1990 levels 2008–2012)	Total asset value (billion U.S. dollars at $14 per ton of carbon dioxi⋯
Spain	261	92	41
Sweden	61	92	10
Switzerland	44	92	7
Ukraine	600	100	102
United Kingdom	584	92	92
United States	4957	93	786
	total 14526	average 95	total 2,345

Sources: 1990 emissions data are official numbers reported by governments to the Uni⋯ Nations Climate Change Secretariat; the data are only for CO_2 emissions from combustion fossil fuels (other data are incomplete). Increase the values about one-quarter to account the non-CO_2 gases. For the reported data, see mainly Conference of the Parties (1997, Anr⋯ to the Decisions, p. 60), which was the only complete set of reported data at the time the Ky⋯ Protocol was negotiated; more recent data for most countries are available from the countr⋯ and reported through the Climate Change Secretariat (http://www.unfccc.int/resource). D⋯ for Croatia, Lithuania, Slovenia, and Ukraine are estimated. The "1990" data are adjusted⋯ nonstandard base years adopted by Bulgaria, Hungary, Poland, and Romania (see notes a⋯ discussion in main text).

Notes: The table shows the value of emission permits ("assigned amounts") allocated in ⋯ Kyoto Protocol assuming that permits would trade at about $14 per ton of carbon dioxi⋯ (For comparison, $14 is equivalent to $50 per ton of carbon when measuring only the carb⋯ content of emissions, which is the practice in many studies. $50 per ton is in the middle of ⋯ range of permit prices estimated by a large number of economic models.) In "Kyoto-spea⋯ the allocations are known as "assigned amounts," not emission permits. That linguistic tw⋯ is an effort, in part, to underscore that the allocations are not permanent entitlements. In rea⋯ however, once the amounts are assigned, secured, and traded they will de facto become se⋯ permanent property rights. Property owners will organize to protect their assets, makin⋯ difficult to reallocate the "assigned amounts" in subsequent negotiating rounds. The ini⋯ allocation will sharply constrain the range of possible subsequent allocations; in effect, ⋯ permits will be awarded for longer periods than the five-year budget periods. Thus it is illus⋯ tive to calculate the value of the permits by treating them as semipermanent property. ⋯ "asset value" is computed by calculating the flow of revenue to nations that hold those per⋯ and then comparing it with 8% corporate bonds that would give the same yield. For the ann⋯ revenue flow associated with these asset values divide by 12.5 (i.e., 1/0.08); for the rever⋯ allocation implied during the Kyoto budget period, multiply the annual flow by five.

agreed to allow emission trading. The United States, for example, arrives at the low-cost estimates for complying with the protocol (a mere $100 per household) only if it purchases about three-fourths of its abatement overseas.[3]

In a single act, the Kyoto session created a highly ambitious agreement that requires a completely novel form of international financial trading to succeed, and no consensus on how to implement that scheme. The next rounds will prove Kyoto to have been an aberration—the imaginary can opener, not proof that it is feasible to hand out and secure assets worth trillions of dollars under international law.

Two nascent problems hint at the troubles to come if nations take emission trading seriously. First, by monetizing commitments, emission trading breeds political conflict. The initial allocation creates expectations that the permits will be durable assets—governments might adjust allocations around the margins, but once distributed the permits would become assets that, like other property rights, owners will fight to protect. The fight is already under way as diplomats discover that "technical" issues—of which dozens must still be settled—are becoming hotly contested zero-sum negotiations. A rule that is beneficial to one party must also harm others.

In 1996, for example, the Conference of the Parties to the Framework Convention on Climate Change (FCCC)—the parent agreement to the Kyoto Protocol—decided to allow countries "undergoing the process of transition to a market economy" to use base years other than 1990. Four countries (Bulgaria, Hungary, Poland, and Romania) did so—all chose earlier years, when their economies were stronger and emissions were higher.[4] Because the Kyoto emission targets were set as a fraction of the base year, higher base year emissions result in more modest targets and a greater number of valuable permits. Those nonstandard base years account for $20 billion (14%) of those four countries' permits shown in table 2.1. That technical decision was relatively easy to adopt because it predated the final negotiation

29

in Kyoto and thus nations were largely unaware of the huge sums that would be in play. Today, even less consequential decisions are stuck in gridlock because now—after Kyoto—governments are becoming aware of how much is at stake.

The other looming problem is the huge windfall that accrues to nations whose diplomats are skilled or lucky. Today's worry is Russia and Ukraine. The Kyoto Protocol obliges these countries to freeze emissions at 1990 levels. Yet the most authoritative study of the world energy system and carbon dioxide emissions, conducted by the International Institute for Applied Systems Analysis (IIASA) and the World Energy Council (WEC),[5] shows that Russian and Ukrainian emissions are unlikely to reach that target even in the absence of any global warming policy. Their economies have shriveled and so has combustion of fossil fuels, the main source of greenhouse gas emissions. Many East European nations are in a similar situation. Together, the IIASA/WEC study projects that emissions from the countries of Eastern Europe and the former Soviet Union will remain a total of about 6.3 billion tons of carbon dioxide below the Kyoto caps from 2008 to 2012 (figure 2.1), with the biggest surpluses in Russia and Ukraine. In contrast, the IIASA/WEC analysis suggests that emissions in the West will exceed the Kyoto targets by at least that much unless action is taken to control emissions. Russia and Ukraine could earn $20–$170 billion (perhaps more) by selling their windfall to the Western nations in need.[6] No wonder suspicious environmentalists have dubbed this "hot air" trading.

Few in Kyoto were fully aware of the scale of these transfers because it was not certain that the economic troubles in the East would be as severe and persistent as they now appear. Russia and the others could plausibly argue that they needed the "headroom" of generous targets—so that emission limits would not pinch as their economies recovered and emissions rose. Western negotiators could not be sure how many permits Eastern nations would really need because it is impossible to predict accurately a nation's economic state and emission levels one decade into

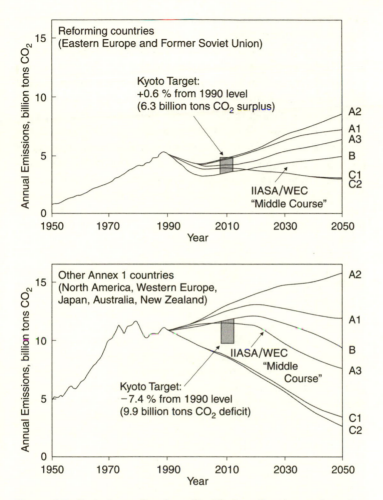

FIGURE 2.1: Emissions of carbon dioxide in reforming nations (top panel) and advanced industrialized countries (bottom panel). The shaded areas show surplus and deficits for the "middle course (B)" scenario published by IIASA/WEC (Nakićenović et al., 1998) and calculated in Victor et al. (2000). Also shown are other IIASA/WEC scenarios for future emissions. The "A" scenarios envision high growth in energy consumption supplied by different fuels and technologies. Emissions

the future. Since Russia, Ukraine, and several other reforming nations were under no domestic pressure to slow global warming, they could easily refuse a deal that was not sweetened with liberal headroom. It is especially interesting that the targets these countries accepted in Kyoto are almost identical to the highest level of emissions that experts thought possible—shown in the "A2" scenario on figure 2.1. In part, that reflects that these reforming nations were especially adamant that they would not accept emission targets that might constrain development of their economies, even in the worst-case scenario where emissions are high. Fear of worst-case scenarios, and the ability to reject inconvenient commitments, gives reluctant participants the power to generate a lot of headroom for the other scenarios that are more likely.

---

are high when coal is king (A2) and lower when carbon-light natural gas dominates (A3). The "C" scenarios envision lower consumption of energy, and lower emissions, partly due to growing concern about the ecological consequences of burning fossil fuels. The two categories of nations shown here (38 individual nations in total) are the only ones required to regulate their emissions within particular binding limits, listed in "Annex B" of the Kyoto Protocol and shown in table 2.1 above. These nations are also often called the "industrialized" nations (in contrast with "developing" nations); governments have never codified the exact requirements that govern the list, such as the level of economic development. Rather, the list is a product of negotiation that, in essence, treats the members of the Organization for Economic Cooperation and Development (OECD) and the major former centrally planned nations as "industrialized" and the rest as "developing." The listing effort dates to the 1992 Framework Convention on Climate Change, which includes in "Annex I" a list of industrialized countries that must initiate controls on greenhouse gases; in contrast, "non-Annex I" (i.e., developing) countries were given more lenient obligations. The convention's Annex I and the protocol's Annex B are nearly identical. Since 1992, Korea and Mexico have joined the OECD, which would suggest that they should be added to these lists—so far, they have not agreed to that change.

What if every reluctant participant could extract such headroom? That is tomorrow's worry as the diplomats in the advanced industrialized countries struggle with ways to include developing countries within the framework of emission trading. Will those efforts merely proliferate "hot air" headroom that undermines true efforts to control emissions, just as printing money causes inflation that erodes monetary assets?

Bargaining with the Wary: Can Emission Trading Expand to Developing Countries?

The Kyoto targets apply only to 38 industrialized countries—the advanced industrialized nations and the reforming countries. So far, the developing countries have no obligation to control emissions. Nor should they. Current per capita emissions in China, for example, are merely one-tenth those of the United States. Historically, industrialized nations are responsible for nearly all the emissions of greenhouse gases that have slowly accumulated in Earth's atmosphere—causing global warming today and also committing future generations to climate changes that they cannot escape for centuries. Indeed, a small fraction of the carbon dioxide emitted from James Watt's original steam engine still affects the climate system today.

Inevitably, however, any serious effort to control global emissions must involve developing countries. These nations are increasingly integrated into the world economy—with the benefits of economic globalization they are expected, also, to shoulder some of the costs of efforts to protect the globe. By about 2020 these countries will account for about half of world emissions of greenhouse gases. Thus we must explore the allocation problem not only for today but also to assess whether it will be possible to allocate new permits in the future so that the trading system can expand to include developing countries.

33

The problem of engaging developing countries and its implications for allocation are already in the news. In Kyoto a coalition of developing countries led by China and India adamantly refused to accept limits on emissions; they even excised language from the Protocol that would have urged voluntary limits. That is why, with the ink on the Kyoto pact barely dry, the U.S. government started waging what Secretary of State Madeleine Albright called a "diplomatic full court press to encourage meaningful developing country participation" in the effort to limit emissions of greenhouse gases.[7] A 1997 U.S. Senate resolution, adopted 95-0, declared dead on arrival any pact that does not include "specific scheduled commitments" for developing countries; a 1998 Senate budget resolution underscored that the Kyoto Protocol failed to meet that test.[8] And an advertising campaign bankrolled by big carbon—mining conglomerates and a few oil companies—has reminded American voters that the Kyoto pact "isn't global and can't work." The Government thus knows that Kyoto will fail if developing countries appear to get a free ride.

At the fourth Conference of the Parties to the FCCC ("COP-4")—the first high-level meeting held after Kyoto, which was convened in Buenos Aires—U.S. diplomats declared the first victories from their full court press. Argentina and Kazakhstan announced that they would adopt binding commitments. In the words of Stuart Eizenstat and Frank Loy, the top State Department officials responsible for global warming policy at the time, these commitments were proof that developing countries realized that putting off action on global warming would be a "costly disaster" that would "strangle growth and devastate the environment."[9] The announcements, U.S. diplomats seemed to hope, were evidence that the Kyoto pact could be salvaged.

The real significance of the Argentine and Kazakh commitments is that they will force negotiators to confront the problem of how to expand the emission trading system. Argentina and

Kazakhstan did not simply announce that they would *voluntarily* restrict growth in emissions, which is what America's "full court press" actually sought. Rather, by seeking formally *binding* targets these countries want to open the door to emission trading and reap emission permit windfalls like the ones that Russia and Ukraine got in Kyoto.[10]

Thus, handling new entrants raises familiar problems of allocation. In Kyoto, when governments agreed to create the most basic architecture for emission trading, the challenge was to divide a pie among a fixed number of diners. Now new diners are coming to the table, and their demands will intensify and complicate the conflicts over allocation. In Kyoto, negotiators fixed the size of the pie and sliced it up when they agreed on the targets for the 38 advanced industrialized and reforming nations. Adding more countries—Argentina and Kazakhstan today, and others tomorrow—would imply that the pie should be increased proportionally and a new slice cut for each new entrant.

But the new diners, like Russia and Ukraine before, do not arrive with the goal of spending money to slow global warming. Rather, they are reluctant—pushed to the table because the advanced industrialized nations want them there. These reluctant entrants will understandably focus on the worst-case scenario—emissions that rise higher than expected—and demand a large slice with ample headroom.[11] Indeed, such concern probably ensures that the slice demanded by the new entrant will be larger than the increase in the total size of the pie that was made to accommodate its arrival. Whereas starting the trading system required solving a difficult zero-sum negotiation in which countries allocated parts of a fixed pie, expanding it to include these new entrants requires an even more intractable negative-sum allocation. The demands of each new entrant imply shrinking the pie left for the incumbents. Simply caving in to these demands by awarding large slices—as with Russia and Ukraine—only temporarily defers the problems. Awarding headroom is akin to rewarding dissidents with newly printed money. "Printing" headroom undermines the value of permits owned by incumbents—permit owners will figure that out quickly and oppose ratification of any mere permit-printing deal. It also undermines environmental quality since costless headroom permits crowd out bona fide efforts to control emissions. So far negotiators have been able to agree in principle on the need for emission trading only because they have never attempted to set general rules for how the system would expand to include other countries.

Emission trading enthusiasts argue that any agreement to slow global warming must allocate benefits and burdens—it is no harder to solve this problem within an architecture based on emission trading than for other architectures. Rather, enthusiasts claim, emission trading could actually ease the problem of allocation. Extra permits could be given to compensate reluctant countries for the cost of adhering to international rules, just as compensation has been important to achieving success in other areas of international cooperation.[12] Permit allocations could be used to offset inequalities in the world economic system—the existence of such inequalities is often used to bolster developing countries' arguments against paying for costly emission controls.

I examine these arguments in two ways. First, I finish the drama started by Argentina and Kazakhstan—will it be possible to print new permits to entice developing countries into the system? My answer is negative, in part because it is so difficult to estimate and agree upon how many permits the new entrants will need for their entire economies. Thus I also explore whether new entrants might earn permits on a project-by-project basis, rather than trying to recruit whole nations. Project-by-project credits are included in the Kyoto Protocol through the Clean Development Mechanism (CDM), and trading enthusiasts see them as a way for developing countries to join a trading system gradually. In essence, the CDM allows fuller trading to emerge from the bottom up, rather than requiring a full allocation of new permits to all participants at the outset.

Permits as Compensation

No doubt, compensation is necessary and can be highly effective in getting reluctant countries to participate in international co-operation, and thus any instrument that eases the process of compensation could make the international effort to slow global warming much more effective. Indeed, compensation has been critical to many of the success stories in international environmental cooperation, such as the highly effective international agreements to protect the ozone layer. Nearly all developing countries have adopted stringent obligations to eliminate their use of ozone-depleting substances, and most developing countries are on track to comply with most of their obligations. Threats of trade sanctions explain some of this behavior, but the most important factor is the Multilateral Fund (MLF) that compensates developing countries for the "agreed incremental costs" of projects that replace ozone-depleting substances with more benign (but often more costly) substitutes. To date, about $1 billion has been committed to projects to cut ozone-depleting substances.

When addressing the global warming problem, however, few observers think that it would be politically feasible to follow the MLF model and simply compensate all developing countries for the full cost of membership in an international global warming treaty. Absent a looming climatic catastrophe, the price tag for full compensation—perhaps hundreds of billions of dollars per year or more just to stabilize emissions from developing countries at current levels—would be too large for legislatures in the industrialized world to stomach. (For comparison, the current level of official development assistance totals less than $50 billion annually for all purposes.) That is why the unwritten code in the United States' effort to obtain "meaningful participation of developing countries" in the Kyoto Process is not only that these countries should adopt significant commitments but also that they should pay part of the bill.

Nonetheless, the possibility that a greenhouse gas emission trading system might some day exist has fed a torrent of theoretical studies that explore how various allocation schemes can make possible an intriguing array of agreements. One strong theme in these studies is that permit allocations can promote world justice—for example, allocating permits on a per capita basis can provide an egalitarian foundation for protecting the atmosphere that is missing in the rest of world politics. Developing nations could earn resources by leasing their excess to the North.[13] Past wrongs can be righted; the true past and future contributors to global warming can finally be held accountable.

These schemes for promoting justice through compensation defy the practical experience with emission trading, which strongly suggests that permits will be grandfathered with small adjustments to account for differences in the willingness to pay for the collective effort. Countries seized by the fear of global warming will accept fewer permits and higher costs than countries, such as Russia, where the population thinks it might even benefit from slightly higher temperatures, longer growing seasons, and a carbon-rich atmosphere that makes some plants grow faster. Envisioning utopian futures where every man, woman, and child has the same permit allocation can help frame long-term goals, but they are not likely to be adopted in the architecture of clear, legally binding targets and timetables that is necessary for an emission trading system to function properly. Some legal theorists have suggested that, all else equal, "fair" agreements are more likely to earn consent and to be effective. But the evidence for that argument is actually not strong, especially in the global warming case where all else is not equal between "fair" and "unfair" allocations.[14] "Fair" allocations, such as on a per capita basis, are necessarily deviations from the status quo arrangement in which existing emitters receive a more generous allocation. Even if nations and peoples could agree on "fairness," implementing a "fair" solution would require a long-term contract between those whose participation is most essential over the short run (industrialized nations that currently have high per capita emissions) and those who must be engaged for collective action to be effective over the long run (developing countries). Since international law is poorly suited to securing long-term inviolable contracts, the short run dominates.

Permits as Rewards

Perhaps the problems of allocating permits to new participants could be eased if allocation did not require estimating the future level of emissions for the entire economy of the new entrant. That task is especially Herculean for the developing countries because data and methods for projecting future emissions in developing countries are especially poor. Moreover, the most important developing countries (e.g., China) could grow quickly—with potentially rapid growth in emissions as well—leading to large demands for headroom. An alternative strategy is to let countries opt in to the trading system if they implement projects that reduce emissions. This approach, in principle, ensures that permits are awarded only for real reduction efforts—in contrast, successful efforts to gain headroom, such as Russia's allocation in Kyoto, can yield many permits even when a country does not change its behavior.

Most discussion of project-by-project crediting in developing countries has occurred within the context of the Kyoto Protocol's Clean Development Mechanism, a renamed and updated version of the FCCC's concepts of activities implemented jointly and joint implementation (AIJ/JI). For simplicity, I refer to the basic concept as the "CDM," although it may be renamed again in the future.

The CDM is important because it encourages investment in economies where emission control is least costly and where investments in new technologies today can "lock in" cleaner development paths that will persist into the future. But there should be no illusion—the CDM is a second-best mechanism. It exists because emissions from developing countries are growing rapidly and thus any significant effort to control world emissions must include action in the developing countries. Climate change is the consequence of total world emissions—it does not matter where those emissions actually occur. Yet most developing countries have adamantly refused to undertake emission control efforts because they want to spend resources on more pressing problems.

While the CDM is understandably important, it will never be very efficient and probably will be much less active than is widely expected today.[15] There will be severe problems in determining baselines against which investors will earn credits—in integrated economies and firms it is nearly impossible to determine what level of emissions would have occurred without a particular investment project. Skepticism that the CDM system leads to real reductions will abound, and the skeptics will demand intense oversight of CDM crediting to ensure that only new and additional investments earn credits and that crediting is not overly generous. That oversight will raise the cost and uncertainty for CDM investors, severely dampening the incentives to invest. Indeed, real experience with CDM-like mechanisms in the United States—notably the "offset" and other clean air programs of the late 1970s and 1980s—suggests that the bureaucratic process of determining baselines and estimating the credits due for "additional" efforts beyond the baseline can introduce large transaction costs that make it unlikely that the CDM will realize more than a small fraction of its potential. Similarly, real experience with the pilot phase of the FCCC's JI program suggests that bureaucratic review has greatly dampened the incentive to invest.[16]

Strategies for Engaging Developing Countries

Thus it is hard to engage reluctant participants within an emission trading system, and that will make it hard to expand the Kyoto framework to include developing countries. Neither of the two strategies explored here is attractive. First, pure compen-

sation—such as by awarding permits to reluctant participants—
is problematic both because it is difficult to know how many
new permits to allocate and because the new entrants will make
excessive demands to hedge against uncertain futures. As incumbents learn about trading they will realize that allocating
extra permits to reluctant participants is identical to printing
money. So far, the Kyoto process has produced little discussion
of this problem only because most of the participants have not
focused on the values at stake and all the difficult decisions
about emission trading rules have been deferred. Second, in
principle the project-by-project mechanisms of the CDM could
engage new countries in exchange for actual projects, rather
than by simply printing money. The CDM is important—without
it there will be no way to create incentives for firms to invest in
low-cost projects to control emissions in developing countries.
In practice, however, these mechanisms will be costly and cumbersome to operate.

Many of these same problems—such as crafting compensation
packages—are not unique to emission trading. They will arise
in any effort to create a truly global solution to global warming.
Thus, before moving on, it is worth focusing on how "global"
the solution must be to be effective.

A growing conventional wisdom holds that all major participants must be involved at the beginning of an effort to control
emissions. Once engaged, all these actors can then deepen their
cooperation and ratchet up the stringency of their limits on
emissions—a strategy known as "broad then deep." This conventional wisdom guides many of Kyoto's critics (especially in
America) who decry the fact that the Kyoto Protocol regulates
only the emissions of the industrialized countries and gives developing countries a free ride. "Broad then deep," Kyoto's critics
maintain, would level the playing field, which they argue is essential. With this conclusion in mind, the debate over the best
instruments for compensation has followed. But is the conclusion valid?

Experts say that breadth before depth is needed to address the problem of "leakage." Limits on the emission of greenhouse gases impose additional costs on some producers of goods and services. Economic activity, and the emissions it causes, "leak" to zones where costs are lower because limits on greenhouse gases are lax or nonexistent. As the separate free trade rules of the World Trade Organization (WTO) open world markets to investment and trade, it becomes easier to shift investment; the dangers of leakage mount.

So long as limits on greenhouse gas emissions remain modest, leakage is probably a much overstated fear. Modest controls on emissions of greenhouse gases are unlikely to have much effect on where firms locate their business. Similar arguments warned of "industrial flight" if nations opened their borders and kept tight labor and environmental regulations in place; yet the evidence has demonstrated that, in general, industrial flight has not been as severe as the flight hypothesis suggested.[17] If nations tighten greenhouse gas controls, however, leakage could be significant. The problem would not exist if all WTO members adopted the same rules for regulating greenhouse gases, but that outcome is unlikely since the willingness to pay for greenhouse gas abatement varies dramatically across the 135 countries that are members of the WTO.

The only solution to the leakage problem is to fix it at the source. Only by bringing the incentives of these two separate regimes—global warming and the WTO—into line can nations align the costs of regulating greenhouse gases with the benefits of free trade. Linking the two will require discriminating between countries according to the intensity with which their production processes emit greenhouse gases, which will erase the classic distinction in trade law between products and processes. Historically, trade law has allowed countries to impose some discrimination on imports according to the characteristics of the *products* themselves—nations may bar hazardous foods, for example. But trade laws forbid discrimination merely on the *pro-*

cess used to make identical end products—for example, allowing steel imports from clean production lines but restricting imports from producers that use more pollution-intensive processes. In reality, however, the product-process distinction is already eroding. In the 1998 "shrimp-turtle" dispute the WTO supported process discrimination if necessary to support a legitimate international environmental objective.[18] The WTO, therefore, is poised to help address this problem, and it is the right forum for doing so.

Thus trading should not be saddled with solving the "leakage" problem—nor can any other system that is focused only on controlling emissions. The problem of "leakage" is not only a product of differential rules for emissions but also the unsustainable wall that has been erected between "environmental" agreements, such as the Kyoto Protocol, and the rules that constitute the international institutions for managing investment and trade in goods and services. The wall is already eroding.

Moreover, critics of the agreements that focus on industrialized countries have not considered the dangers of their "broad" strategy. In particular, starting with "broad" regulatory commitments risks perpetual shallowness. International agreements with many parties are often unwieldy because near universal consent is needed to adopt collective decisions, including decisions on critical institutions and procedures. Moreover, it is especially difficult to achieve unanimous agreements that surpass the lowest common denominator when the number of parties is large and interests diverge. Compensation and differential commitments can help break this tendency, but such rules are complicated and difficult to design—multiplying the number of parties escalates the challenge.

Particularly worrisome is the fact that broad agreements rarely lead to strong enforcement mechanisms because they often encompass a large number of parties that fear being held accountable for their commitments; those wary parties scuttle any serious effort to adopt an enforcement mechanism.[19] Without enforcement available, it is difficult to establish firm commitments—even enthusiastic participants will be wary of undertaking costly actions unless they know that other major countries (especially their trading partners) are also being held accountable. In contrast, deep agreements among like-minded countries make it easier to gain agreement on strong institutions, which can then be codified into place as participation in the agreement expands.[20] Like-minded countries that cooperate on environmental topics are also typically liberal democracies—their governments are not only under democratic pressure to protect the environment but also already densely engaged with other international institutions and thus more likely to accept the jurisdiction of new, powerful international institutions. The few instances where agreements have combined breadth and depth—for example, the WTO agreements—usually began as narrow agreements among liberal democracies that expanded outwards and became more demanding at the same time.

Is the risk of perpetual shallowness worth the supposed benefits of an agreement with broad participation? The optimal approach may be to pursue both strategies at the same time. On this score, the United Nations Framework Convention on Climate Change (UNFCCC), the parent agreement of the Kyoto Protocol, may be partially on the right track. Data gathering and review functions are pursued at the global level, and developing countries are compensated for the incremental costs of participating in those global activities. It makes little sense to lay a baseline of data for a global problem unless almost all countries provide data. (It is a pity, however, that the rules governing the data collection process are particularly elastic for the developing nations, and thus the accuracy and comparability of the data gathered are likely to be poor.) Meanwhile, efforts to regulate emissions under the UNFCCC focus more narrowly on the many fewer nations that are committed to action. These are mainly the advanced liberal democracies that have already accepted a wide range of international legal agreements and are generally comfortable with the idea that demanding and intrusive international institutions are necessary for addressing collective problems.[21]

Thus clear thinking is needed on the participation strategy—regardless of whether emission trading is included as a central element of an international agreement for slowing global warming. To some degree, the dilemmas of trading are separate from the choice of participation strategy. But the problems of initial allocation and adjustment of permit allocations greatly complicate any participation strategy. The "broad then deep" strategy is difficult to follow because it is extremely difficult to achieve the omnibus allocation of permits among the dozens of countries that would be included. The "deep then broad" strategy makes more sense—not only for trading but also for any other serious international effort that requires hard choices about rules and allocations. Although the "deep then broad" strategy would ease the "cold start" problem of initially allocating permits to many dozens of countries, it would limit expansion of the trading system to the very slow pace of CDM-like mechanisms.

Are Domestic Trading Programs Useful Models?

Trading enthusiasts point to several successful national trading programs—particularly in the United States—as proof that the allocation problems can be solved and that the elegant theory of emission trading can be put into actual practice. That experience suggests many important lessons that must be applied to the design of an international emission trading program, such as the importance of low transaction costs, strict monitoring and enforcement, and the need to minimize interventions on the part of administrators that cause instability and uncertainty in markets. But on two critical issues—the allocation of permits, and the "banking" and "borrowing" of permits over time—the *differences* between international and national trading systems matter much more than the similarities.

The most frequently cited success story is the U.S. sulfur trading system, which is halving the total emissions of sulfur dioxide that cause acid rain. In that case, U.S. lawmakers successfully allocated permits because they could credibly threaten to impose other, more costly regulatory alternatives such as "command-and-control" technology standards or a tax on emissions. Faced with this choice, major emitting firms (electric utilities) quickly lined up to support emission trading. They generally favored market-based solutions like taxes or permits over less efficient command-and-control regulation. And they preferred permits to taxes because the permits would be distributed mainly in proportion to past emissions. Grandfathering gave existing emitters an asset (the permits) and control over the revenue from trading; emission taxes, in contrast, would be more harmful to the status quo because all emitters would be taxed and revenues would flow to the government. Instead of the status quo giveaway, many economists favored requiring firms to bid for permits at an auction. But auctions were politically unattractive for the same reasons that emitters abhorred emission taxes—they would impose severe costs on the status quo.

Not all stakeholders favored trading over the alternatives. Miners of high-sulfur coal favored command-and-control regulations that would require utilities to install scrubbers, which might have preserved the market for their coal and made it difficult for utilities to switch to less sulfurous western coals. But they were outvoted. Senator Byrd—the political patriarch of West Virginia, a major producer of high-sulfur coals—organized a package of job retraining programs that partially compensated the miners and softened the opposition.[22]

Imagine how different sulfur regulation would have been if every sulfur-emitting firm could veto any significant rule that harmed its interests. Broadly, that is the context in which the Kyoto Protocol would operate under international law. Treaties, the main instruments of international law, require consent (ratification) by all of the states that are bound. The requirement of universal consent makes it extremely difficult to implement any scheme that is both stringent and harmful to some interests. While there are many linkages and pressures that push countries to join international agreements, a country's choice to bind itself still depends mainly on whether it is individually better off inside the agreement than outside. That is why international law is weak and conservative—an instrument for negotiating and codifying unanimous views, but unable to impose decisions that harm a significant minority. That calculus leads to the familiar tragedy of the commons—society as a whole would benefit from collective action, but cooperation fails because each member is individually better off by defection. All international cooperation on global warming faces this challenge, but a permit system is especially sensitive to the inability to impose international legal decisions. The wonder of market-based trading is based on the fact that permits are valuable, but the permits sustain value only if permits are scarce, the market inspires confidence, and major permit buyers can continue to justify outlays. In a domestic trading system the center (the government) makes the rules and thus market players have confidence that their rights are secure. But at the international level the center does not exist; security of property rights created by international law is weak. Defection by only a few actors that are dissatisfied with the allocation could quickly unravel the entire trading system.[23]

The problem of collective action has been partially solved by institutions that impose penalties on defectors, but the success stories are few and are not applicable to emission trading. The most successful example from global cooperation is the free trade regime of the General Agreement on Tariffs and Trade (GATT) and World Trade Organization (WTO). However, trade is a reciprocal activity and thus it is relatively easy to enforce trade obligations through retaliation. Indeed, the large GATT/ WTO members—especially the United States—have often threatened and occasionally applied reciprocity to force compliance. Multilateral institutions such as WTO's Dispute Settlement

Body (DSB) have made enforcement more evenhanded by focusing retaliation on only true violations and, to a lesser degree, by making it easier for small states to enforce compliance.

However, the DSB experience is not directly relevant to emission trading. Unlike trade in goods and services, emission trading cannot rely directly on reciprocity and retaliation. Reciprocity is not effective in fluid commodity markets that have many buyers and sellers. For example, if Russia flouted the rules and other countries did the same in retaliation then the problem would only worsen because the market would be flooded with bogus permits. Like inflation, excess fluidity would degrade the value of bona fide permits and give everyone—cheaters and boy scouts alike—an incentive to abandon the system. Other areas of international cooperation, such as international environmental law, are more similar to the collective action problem that a trading system must confront, but the experience in those systems has been poor—enforcement mechanisms are nonexistent or weak. We will return to the enforcement problem in chapter 3.

The other way that international trading differs markedly from the national experience is in the "borrowing" and "banking" of permits. Such transfers over time—especially banking—are allowed under many domestic permit systems and appear to have helped lower the cost of meeting environmental objectives.

Borrowing could be important because several studies have suggested that the most efficient way to regulate greenhouse gas emissions would be to allow emissions to remain high over the next few decades, followed by steep cuts in the future, when low-cost carbon-free technologies will be less costly.[24] Borrowing permits from the future could allow that to happen. But borrowing has been explicitly rejected in the Kyoto Protocol, and for good reason: One can't borrow unless the rules that govern future allocation are settled. Indeed, Kyoto allocated permits only for a five-year period—2008 to 2012—and explicitly did not attempt a longer-term allocation. That single-period allocation has, *de facto*, set the stage for later periods; but an explicit multiperiod allocation would have been much more difficult to achieve because the stakes would have been much higher. It might be possible to allow borrowing without first achieving an omnibus multiperiod allocation if international law could ensure that borrowed permits would be deducted from future allocations. But international law requires universal consent and is therefore very poor at sending credible long-term signals. Parties could borrow to the hilt and then withdraw. Heavy borrowing would simply adjust the starting point for negotiating future allocations, which become inflated to offset the "borrowed" permits.

In principle, banking unused permits for use in future periods should be easier to implement because it rewards actions rather than promises. In practice, however, banking is unlikely to be substantial for the same reason that borrowing would be highly efficient—in most cases it is cheaper to defer rather than to accelerate controls on emissions. Nonetheless, there is a possibility that banking could play a significant role, which is why Article 3.13 of the Kyoto Protocol explicitly envisions it. For example, banking could greatly reduce the political and environmental problem of Russian and Ukrainian "hot air." Those countries would no longer gain a costless windfall by selling their permits if they had the option of banking them for the future.

In reality, the political process for establishing international legal commitments strongly penalizes banking. Amounts held for the future have the political effect of announcing that past allocations have been too generous. The banker thus weakens his hand in future negotiations. As any bureaucrat skilled at protecting his budget knows, spending—not banking—is the dominant behavior when assets are allocated in a multiround process that is not guided by inviolable principles. Russia and Ukraine will pocket the billions in cash or other secure assets rather than risk losing their windfall while waiting for the day when the permits might actually be needed to cover Russian and Ukrainian emissions.

Summary and Assessment

Allocation is the big problem with emission trading. The success in solving allocation problems in some national trading systems does not yield relevant lessons for international emission trading—within national systems the central government can impose solutions on reluctant parties, but at the international level there is no central authority that binds the wary. Allocation problems are already arising in the Kyoto Protocol, and they loom large as diplomats contemplate how to involve developing countries in an emission trading system. Broadly, the allocation problems are threefold.

First, a lot is at stake because a permit system involves the trading of assets (permits), not just the coordination of the annual cost of controlling emissions. By monetizing those assets the system makes the stakes highly transparent and magnifies political conflicts during both the allocation of permits and the setting of rules that will govern the permit system. The calculation here suggests that the permits might be worth about $2 trillion; that value, which includes only permits for emissions of carbon dioxide from the combustion of fossil fuels, would be higher by perhaps one-quarter if it had included other greenhouse gases. (I address the fluxes of other gases in the next chapter.) If negotiators in Kyoto had attempted to allocate quotas to developing countries the total value would be higher still.

Although a few trillion dollars is a lot of money, it is not incomparable with valuations for other major assets in modern economies. Today's heady stock markets suggest that the total value of publicly traded companies is about $30 trillion.[25] America's $786 billion of emission permits (table 2.1) is about equal to the market capitalization of Intel, Microsoft and Oracle. Nor are the amounts awarded in Kyoto incomparable with the total value of public lands in America. Since the formation of the United States, about 2 billion acres of land have been public domain; the Federal government has sold or given away a total of about 1.2 billion acres through sundry programs such as the 1862 Homestead Act.[26] If those lands were worth $1000 per acre today the total distribution would be of comparable value to the Kyoto pact. Nor are the values incomparable with other public assets sold at auction—for example, the United Kingdom is raising about $35 billion in its auction of "third-generation" mobile phone licenses,[27] or about one-third the value of its Kyoto allocation.

In short, the valuations of greenhouse gas permits could be extremely large, but they are comparable with valuations in other major aspects of economic policy. If global warming were viewed as a serious problem—one of the central problems of modern times—the sheer magnitude of the permits alone might not be an insurmountable obstacle to creating a trading system. But we should not be sanguine—Intel, Microsoft, Oracle, and the public land distributions were amassed through thousands of individual decisions, rather than as the products of an international treaty from which any dissatisfied party could defect.

Second, cold starting a trading program will probably result in massive financial flows. Those could be inefficient if they are squandered in the world economy (e.g., in the hands of corrupt Russian oligarchs). And they will cause huge political problems as the countries that are likely to supply those flows ponder whether to ratify their commitments and join a trading system. The problem arises because it is impossible to estimate future emission levels and abatement costs accurately and thus impossible to allocate permits exactly on lines of equal marginal cost. Negotiators might reduce the technical problem by shortening the time that passes between the negotiation of permit allocations and the start of the trading system and by beginning with less stringent targets. Both those reforms would make it easier to estimate emissions and abatement costs and thus politically easier to reach a bargain sufficiently durable that the trading system could begin. The instinct of diplomats and governments, however, is to lengthen and stretch. At Kyoto, they decided that

51

a whole decade would pass before their fanciful targets would take hold. Realistic targets that took effect in half that time would have been a better strategy.

Even if technical obstacles to allocating permits along lines of equal cost could be overcome, political barriers remain. Countries that care little about global warming and fear that emission caps might be costly will demand additional permits or refuse to participate. Once the market begins operation and the permits trade to equalize marginal costs, the surplus will be sold to high cost countries and yield financial flows. The controversy over "hot air"—the surplus allocations for Russia and Ukraine—is a particular illustration of the general problem.

This problem is most severe when the regime is expanded to include countries that are least willing to control emissions as well as countries whose economies and energy systems are difficult to predict because they are undergoing massive transformation. The problem for trading is that those attributes describe not only Russia and Ukraine but also nearly all countries in the developing world. Far from providing an easy way to compensate reluctant participants and create a broad regulatory regime, the trading instrument assures that nations must contend with the thorny political problem of how to handle large financial flows before they can "cold start" the system.

The European Union has proposed a solution: to limit the use of trading to 50% of a country's total emission cap, thus ensuring that "hot air" (and warm air) does not flood the market and reduce the incentives for firms in advanced industrialized countries to undertake emissions controls.[28] But that solution would only worsen the situation because countries would fill their trading quota with the cheapest permits—the "hot air" headroom, which costs nothing to print—thus squeezing more expensive credits that represent real reductions in emissions from the market. Bad assets chase good ones from the market. Instead, the proper remedy is to build a trading system with a limited number of participants that have similar willingness to pay for abatement—a "deep" regime, rather than a "broad" one.

Third, the conventional solution to the problem of allocation has been to "grandfather" the permits to existing emitters. Politically, that approach has worked well in national trading systems because it awards valuable assets to the same stakeholders that would otherwise most strongly oppose limits on emissions. But that approach is not politically sustainable for an international greenhouse gas trading program. Developing countries adamantly oppose grandfathering on the basis of current emissions because emissions from developing nations are rising rapidly. In contrast, emissions from industrialized nations—which are today's top emitters—are increasing at a much slower pace, and in some industrialized nations (notably Germany and the United Kingdom) emissions are actually declining. Yet if diplomats envision eventually imposing tight limits on emissions of greenhouse gases then they must also have a plan for allocating commitments in a way that is acceptable to developing countries. Diplomats could make special allocations to satisfy those countries' interests, but any deviation from the status quo would harm existing interests in the industrialized nations. Nor would it be technically and politically easy to compute the size of the extra allocation—too generous an allocation would increase "hot air," and one too stingy would deter developing countries from joining. Shortening the time between negotiation and implementation of the agreement might ease the technical and political challenges, as suggested above. However, short time horizons do not give firms the long-term signals that promote innovation and efficient emission control with the turnover of the capital stock.

Allocation is a Gordian knot. One can devise clever ways to untie parts of the problem, but only by entangling others. One could cut through the knot with a "Rawlsian" negotiation that distributed permanent entitlements for all nations or peoples, but those solutions are difficult to implement in the real world where nations defect from international legal agreements that impose unfavorable short-term allocations. In a crisis these problems might be solved. The appearance of a solution in Kyoto, however, is not evidence that diplomats can devise a politically durable scheme for allocating trillions of dollars through international law. Rather, it is evidence that diplomats are skilled at deferring decisions on difficult questions.

CHAPTER 3
Monitoring and Enforcement

Once permits are allocated, emission trading requires monitoring and enforcement. A permit that allows one ton of CO_2 emission per year might cost approximately $10 to $20 per year.[1] The average American, directly or indirectly, would need permits to cover about 20 tons of emissions annually. Who would purchase such costly permits unless they were sure that a permit was needed to cover every ton?

Because monitoring and enforcement of international legal obligations are such difficult and perennial problems, one school of legal thinking deserves special attention before we begin. It argues that compliance with international agreements is often high, and willful violations are few, because governments tend to obey international law. The norm in favor of following international laws exerts a strong "pull" on behavior, and it is easier for governments to conform than devise crafty ways to skirt international obligations.[2] If this school is correct then perhaps the need for strict monitoring and enforcement is overblown.

In reality, this school is a very poor guide for designing an emission trading system; nor did the school's architects ever intend to have their findings used for this purpose.[3] The evidence that compliance with international obligations is high is drawn mainly from advanced democratic nations replete with environmental NGOs and other public interest groups that pressure their governments to comply.[4] Moreover, compliance has been highest when commitments were trivial or modest; this has been the experience under most international environmental accords.[5]

Global warming will be different. For most industrial nations, meeting the Kyoto targets will be costly and will affect their economic competitiveness. Permits could be worth trillions of dollars; incentives to cheat will be strong. Many (if not all) governments would distribute emission permits to private firms and individuals, which would make the trading system more efficient but would also complicate the task of ensuring compliance. Monitoring and enforcement cannot be left to the honor system.

Monitoring Emissions

In most international environmental agreements, monitoring begins with data in reports that are submitted by the parties themselves.[6] On-site inspection is rare; independent data that might be needed to verify compliance are seldom sought or used. Some exceptions exist, as in several international wildlife agreements that often make use of independent data (e.g., supplied by NGOs).[7] For example, the independently managed system for tracking shipments under the Convention on International Trade in Endangered Species—one of the most successful international programs for monitoring compliance with an environmental treaty—is able to identify a small (but growing) fraction of the total number of suspected violations.[8] Filling data gaps requires either pleading with governments or well-developed networks of nongovernmental organizations that, typically without legal powers, are able to infiltrate illegal trade activities and gather the needed data. The experience with data reporting under the Montreal Protocol on Substances that Deplete the Ozone Layer has been largely successful because data are easy to gather and report and developing countries receive compensation for the full cost of data reporting programs; nonetheless, there have been several cases of suspicious data and the international institutions are largely powerless to prosecute them.[9] In none of the multilateral environmental agreements has self-reporting, by itself, resulted in accurate databases of the sort that most experts think will be necessary for a properly functioning emission trading market. For comparison, the U.S. sulfur dioxide trading program includes a system of continuous emission monitors that provide emissions data that is accurate within a few percent, and government regulators have powerful inspection rights if they need additional information.

Monitoring would not be a severe problem if an emission trading system were restricted to carbon dioxide emitted from fossil fuels. Nearly all fossil fuels are traded in commercial markets and thus in most countries there are multiple, independent data sources already available. The quantity of carbon dioxide emitted during the combustion of fossil fuels is the direct consequence of the well-known quantity of carbon in the fuels themselves; emission factors have been studied intensively and are well known. As illustrated in figure 1.1, different data sets produce consistent emission estimates. Not only would a system that includes only carbon dioxide from fossil fuels be easy to monitor, it would also be quite effective: that source has been responsible for 70% of the global warming since preindustrial times (table 3.1) and is expected to account for a similar fraction in the future. Some on-site inspection would still be needed, especially in countries that have poor fossil fuel accounting systems and that consume large quantities of their own fossil fuel production internally (e.g., Russia). Creating such an inspection system would be difficult but probably not impossible.

TABLE 3.1
Sources and Sinks of Gases Regulated by the Kyoto Protocol

Gas (% warming since preindustrial era)	Source or sink (billion metric tons per year)	Measurement uncertainty	Change in measurement uncertainty (after source/sink is regulated)
Carbon dioxide (70%)			
Combustion of fossil fuels	20000	10%	unchanged
Land use changes, tropical	5900	60%	unknown; possibly low
Land use changes, northern hemisphere	-3000	100%	unknown
Methane (20%)			
Fossil fuel production	100	20% to 30%	slightly lower
Rice paddies	60	70% to 150%	higher uncertainty
Animal waste gases	105	20%	unchanged
Sewage treatment and landfills	55	30% to 130%	slightly lower
Biomass burning	40	50% to 100%	unchanged
Nitrous oxide (6%)			
Soils	5	100%	unchanged or higher
Biomass burning	2	70%	unchanged or higher
Combustion of fossil fuels	2	50%	unchanged
Nylon and fertilizer production	2	30%	lower
Hydrofluorocarbons (<1%)			
Byproduct of CFC and semiconductor manufacture (HFC-23)	?	?	much lower
Refrigerant (HFC-134a)	?	?	much lower
Sulfur hexafluoride (1%)			
Insulator in high-voltage electrical equipment	0.0046	30%	lower
Magnesium casting	0.0012	50%	lower
Perfluorocarbons (1%)			
Aluminum smelting (CF$_4$)	0.015	30%	lower
Semiconductor manufacture (CF$_4$)	0.00057	100%	much lower

Notes and Sources: CO_2 from fossil fuels includes the CO_2 source due to cement manufacturing. Only the major hydrofluorocarbons (HFCs) and perfluorocarbons (PFCs) are shown—other HFCs and PFCs are at present extremely minor players. Measurement uncertainty is the uncertainty *worldwide* emission estimates based on reports of the Intergovernmental Panel on Climate Change (especially Schimel et al. 1996). Except for fossil fuel CO_2, typically national measurement statistics are more uncertain than the worldwide figures unless national data are backed by an extensive ground-up measurements (e.g., forest inventories in the United States, Finland, and other countries). Many industrialized countries have such inventory programs in place or under advanced development, but the author is unaware of any detailed analysis of the accuracy of emissions from those programs compared with the accuracy of worldwide estimates. Uncertainty "after regulation" indicates whether measurement problems will improve or deteriorate after countries and firms put cost-effective policies into place to regulate emissions—estimates based on the author's assessment of the literature. Estimates for HFCs, PFCs, and sulfur hexafluoride are from Victor and MacDonald (1999).

But the Kyoto Protocol is not restricted to carbon dioxide emitted from fossil fuels. It explicitly includes emissions of five other greenhouse gases. In addition, it also includes carbon dioxide fluxes that result from changes in land use—for example, growing trees absorb carbon dioxide (half the mass of wood is carbon), and countries can earn a credit for such "sinks."

The logic for a multigas and multisource approach is impeccable: set environmental goals like slowing global warming in the most encompassing terms possible, and give market actors the flexibility to choose among as many strategies as possible for meeting them. The logic, however, ignores reality: expanding the trading system beyond carbon dioxide emitted from fossil fuels hugely complicates the problem of monitoring. Take the case of methane. Measured worldwide, the major anthropogenic sources of methane are uncertain by 20% to 150% (table 3.1). Atmospheric measurements can be used to determine the total net source of methane quite accurately. But accurately determining the different sources—rice paddies, fossil fuel production, cow belching, etc.—is more difficult. Moreover, what matters most for determining compliance with international legal agreements such as the Kyoto Protocol are national emissions because commitments are set nation by nation. Yet measurement at fine levels of geographical resolution often raises uncertainty. Ground-level programs, such as sampling at individual coal mines or rice paddies, can help determine the relative magnitude of sources, but sampling is imperfect and emissions often depend heavily on local conditions that cannot be easily and systematically measured worldwide or nationwide. For example, methane emissions from irrigated rice fields, measured from seedling to harvest, vary up to thirtyfold within a single country.[10]

The ability to monitor some sources of these gases may actually worsen in the future because the most cost-effective ways to control some emissions will be extremely difficult to monitor. Methane emitted from rice paddies, for example, can be cut by over half with simple changes in the type and timing of fertilizer application. Simply draining irrigated fields once at midseason can cut emissions by 50%; studies in the United States suggest that multiple well-timed drainings can cut emissions by nearly 90%.[11] These are subtle behavioral changes, for which it is easy to claim credit but difficult for outsiders to verify. Unlike emission of carbon dioxide from fossil fuels—where there is an easily measured proxy (quantity of a particular fossil fuel sold) and easily measured emission factors (quantity of emissions per unit of fuel burned)—for most fluxes of methane and nitrous oxide there is no easily measured proxy for emissions and emission factors vary widely.[12]

In principle, including methane and nitrous oxide in a trading system would be valuable—together, these two gases account for about one-quarter of human-caused global warming. But including them comes at high cost to the integrity of a trading system. Studies have shown that firms falsify data and attempt to cheat when international commitments require behavioral changes that are costly and difficult to verify. For example, international rules to regulate discharges of oil from tankers simply barred high discharges and relied on tanker captains' logs for monitoring; they failed because there was no way to verify compliance and the captains rarely incriminated themselves. Far more effective were rules requiring tanker owners and manufacturers to install particular equipment to limit oily discharges. The equipment rules succeeded by ensuring that required changes were easy to verify, difficult to reverse, and needed to take place only once.[13]

Including carbon dioxide fluxes due to changes in land use could also make a trading system more efficient, but measuring these fluxes accurately is especially difficult. Already net growth in trees and plants offsets perhaps one-sixth of the CO_2 emissions due to combustion of fossil fuels (table 3.1); government-reported forest inventories suggest that forests are growing larger and denser in all Annex B nations.[14] Many studies and numerous real-world projects show that managing forests and soils is, in principle, one of the cheapest ways to manage atmospheric carbon. The problem is that at the national level of resolution, which is what matters for commitments under international legal agreements such as the Kyoto Protocol, many countries are unable to monitor carbon dioxide absorbed in trees and soils within a factor of ten. That problem is severe in Russia's Siberian forests, which may account for more of the net flux of forest-related carbon than the forests in any other Annex B country.[15] Even in the United States, recent results suggest that the flux of carbon into forests is uncertain by perhaps a factor of three or more; variability in the net flux from year to year is about 100%.[16] Traders of this new currency may not be able to distinguish a dime from a dollar, or an asset from a liability.

Sorting out these problems will be technically difficult, not least because it is often difficult to distinguish carbon fluxes caused by mankind (and thus included in the Kyoto Protocol) from natural fluxes that diplomats may try to exclude from the Kyoto accounting. Natural ecosystems cause huge sources and sinks of carbon—they absorb carbon through photosynthesis but emit carbon during respiration. What matters for global warming is the net flux, which is much smaller than and highly sensitive to errors in estimating the gross fluxes.[17] Moreover, the natural biosphere is variable and ecosystems are slow to adjust fully. Thus the time required to verify that a change in carbon has actually occurred is probably longer than the five-year Kyoto budget period—perhaps much longer. For example, a research group at the International Institute for Applied Systems Analysis (IIASA) has calculated that verifying the change in emissions from large-scale forestry projects at 90% confidence interval could take five decades.[18] A firm that invests in carbon sequestration might not know the return on its investment until decades after it is needed. Time delays and uncertainty could greatly discount the economic value of sequestration.

The only way to reduce uncertainties in the measured fluxes of methane, nitrous oxide, and biotic carbon dioxide is a pro-

61

gram for collecting independent on-site data. Remote sensing, such as by satellite, is not enough. Satellites can provide information on forest areas, for example, but they are of little help in measuring woody biomass or changes in the quantity of carbon in soils, which is what is important when assessing the total carbon balance. An intrusive monitoring program is technically feasible—soil samples, in situ monitoring, and other techniques could fill the data needs. But politically, the needed monitoring program would be a huge liability. Already the mission to slow global warming has many detractors. A system of UN-sanctioned methane sniffers and soil samplers would multiply their ranks. Especially in America, isolationists fearful of UN regulation would be emboldened if the feared "black helicopters" and snoops of the UN actually existed.

Remarkably, not a single study has adequately examined the critical policy question: does the extra flexibility of extending a trading system beyond fossil fuel emissions of carbon dioxide offset the additional administrative burden and uncertainty? A few studies have shown that achieving a given goal of limiting global warming would be cheaper if several gas fluxes—notably of methane and the biotic absorption of carbon dioxide—were part of the solution, rather than exclusively limiting fossil fuel carbon dioxide.[19] A few studies have examined transaction costs.[20] But no study has done both. My assessment is that it is likely that the benefit of including all gases in a modest regulatory system (e.g., the Kyoto limits) would be swamped by the additional costs for monitoring compliance. The essential rationale for a multigas emission trading—which has been U.S. policy[21] since 1990—is based on elegant theory but scant data and almost no analysis of real-world policy choices.

As with solving the leakage problem, it is likely that the need for a multisource and multigas "comprehensive" approach will be small in the near future but will grow in importance as regulation of greenhouse gases tightens.[22] Until then, the best approach is to sponsor serious technical work on multigas monitoring, collect baseline emission data for multiple gases, and to explore the tradeoffs between single- and multiple-gas regulatory instruments, rather than to attempt to associate valuable emission credits with poorly monitored emissions. If governments ignore this advice and lump all the gases together prematurely they will create strong incentives to jigger the accounts and undermine the long-term viability of the multigas approach. One episode in Kyoto exposed the tip of the iceberg. Delegates agreed to a clause inserted by the Australian government that allows industrialized countries with net positive land-use emissions to include those emissions when they calculate their 1990 base year (Article 3.7). Only Australia would qualify because all other industrialized countries were experiencing a net growth in forests and thus emissions related to land use were negative.[23] A recent study suggests that the "Australia clause" yields perhaps a 19% increase in Australia's 1990 emissions.[24] That 19% windfall created another $10 billion (about $500 for every Australian resident) in assets, in addition to the value shown for Australia in table 2.1.

Self-interested rule making is inevitable. Every regulatory system requires technical decisions that affect interests, inevitably. Those decisions can become politicized. It is especially worrisome, however, that the first efforts to develop technical rules and procedures for monitoring are taking place just at the time when the existence of the Kyoto Protocol makes countries both aware of the huge sums at stake and especially keen to twist rules to their own advantage.

Enforcement

Clearing the hurdles of allocation and monitoring still leaves the need for enforcement. In practice, no demanding legal system— even in a police state—results in 100% compliance. But high levels of compliance and general respect for the rule of law are probably needed to assure the value of permits and the efficiency of the emissions trading system. Such adherence to the law will not come automatically. By putting a dollar value on all emissions, trading makes cheating especially seductive because it is easy for delinquents to spot and cash the rewards of deviance.

The problems of international enforcement are familiar. By itself international law has no police power; most mechanisms that are formally empowered to enforce international legal obligations are cumbersome and inefficient. Even the extensive procedures for enforcement of international norms on human rights, which are often viewed as highly effective, are typically invoked only in major cases, if at all. Less weighty violations are simply ignored or addressed haphazardly.[25] For many multilateral agreements, formal enforcement mechanisms do not exist at all.

In other areas of international environmental law, stakeholders have imagined three "ways around" the dearth of enforcement mechanisms, but in practice none is likely to be very effective for enforcing compliance with an emission trading system. First, in principle it is possible to use dispute resolution procedures to enforce international legal commitments. Most multilateral environmental agreements include these procedures, which are often elaborate. In practice, however, no dispute resolution mechanism in any multilateral environmental treaty has ever been vested with significant powers to resolve conflicts.[26] Nor has any party even invoked a dispute resolution mechanism in a multilateral environmental treaty.[27] Most failures to comply with international environmental obligations cause damages that diffuse to all parties and the environment itself; thus disputes, which are bilateral in character, rarely emerge.

The architects of multilateral environmental agreements have invented "noncompliance procedures" as a remedy. Originally developed under the Montreal Protocol on Substances that Deplete the Ozone Layer, noncompliance procedures are designed to address compliance problems in a multilateral context. They are intended to facilitate compliance and to be nonconfrontational—inviting rather than threatening. In this spirit, the Framework Convention on Climate Change includes a "multilateral consultative process" (Article 13), and the Kyoto Protocol requires the parties to develop "effective procedures and mechanisms" for identifying and handling cases of noncompliance (Article 18). Efforts are under way to develop rules to guide these procedures, although neither is yet in operation. The experience with the Montreal Protocol demonstrates that noncompliance procedures can have some effect, although the mechanism is weak—purposely stripped of any real power except jawboning and persuasion. The weakness is a direct result of the practice adopted in the Montreal Protocol—and replicated in the FCCC and Kyoto Protocol—of negotiating the rules for the compliance procedure *after* setting the treaty commitments. Since the rulemaking process requires unanimous consent, strong compliance mechanisms do not transpire. Indeed, Article 18 of the Kyoto Protocol requires formally amending the Protocol if the parties adopt a compliance mechanism that entails "binding consequences." The efforts to develop rules for Article 18 have been closely focused on creating a procedure that is sufficiently consensual that it may not trigger the requirement for amendment, which would reopen the Protocol's closets, expose the skeletons inside, and accelerate its collapse. Noncompliance procedures do not create rule of law, although they probably help promote higher levels of compliance than would otherwise exist.[28]

Second, mindful of these difficulties, some nations have sought to supplement (or supplant) weak multilateral enforcement with unilateral enforcement actions. For example, the United States has made effective use of threats of economic and diplomatic sanctions against countries that do not comply with international rules on protecting wildlife.[29] However, this approach will not create the evenhanded rule of law that is necessary for an effective permit trading market because systems based on unilateral enforcement are governed by the interests of the enforcers. Moreover, sanctions have proved much less effective when levied against major powers (e.g., the United States), countries that are isolated from trade and thus not especially vulnerable to sanctions (e.g., Russia), or when political linkages such as fear of backlash make sanctioning difficult (e.g., Russia).[30]

Third, nongovernmental organizations (NGOs) might help enforce international legal obligations. Indeed, public interest and industry groups often play a significant role in forcing compliance with agreed norms. In practice, however, NGOs are not evenhanded enforcers—they enforce when it is in their interest to do so, and when they are capable of action.[31] For example, environmental groups have played prominent roles in enforcing international agreements to protect wildlife. But they focus their action on rules that protect panda bears, elephants, tigers, and other "charismatic megafauna" that attract dues-paying members. As a group, public interest NGOs have given much less attention to less charismatic flora, such as endangered cacti. As with wildlife protection, global warming generally attracts public attention, so environmental NGOs are highly active on the topic. The brunt of environmental NGOs' energy is focused on big countries and firms that are politically attractive targets—not on evenhanded enforcement of small and large violations alike.

Perhaps industry NGOs will have a stronger interest in enforcing compliance with an emission permit system. If enforcement is poor, the value of their property rights will degrade. However, each permit holder, individually, would be harmed only a small amount by any particular instance of noncompliance. One could imagine that permit-holders' associations would emerge to overcome this problem of collective action—just as firms often create collective lobbies to advance their interests. But many potential members of such a lobby will be wary of strong, intrusive enforcement and reluctant to join—in general, permit holders will also be emitters and therefore could benefit from poor enforcement. The main problem, however, is collective action. A truly global permit market would diffuse the benefits of enforcement across hundreds of countries and millions (or billions) of permit holders, making collective enforcement difficult to organize.[32]

Even if environmental groups and permit holders could somehow realize their collective interest in enforcing the permit system it is unclear what they could achieve. Some of the data that they would need to prosecute violations—such as emission estimates—are internal to countries and firms and could be difficult to obtain and challenge. In many countries, legal systems are weak or corrupt and thus there is no way to impose enforcement actions on deviant emitters. The country in that situation—which may include most nations on earth—could find that its private actors have collectively violated the country's international obligations by emitting more than the country's permit holdings; yet the government could find it difficult to hold any emitter individually responsible and impossible to bring the country as a whole back into compliance. Governments could help the enforcement process by creating institutions that could scrutinize a country's "internal" policies and create accurate data sets on behavior. But the countries that are least likely to accept international jurisdiction are those whose behavior is most likely to require international intrusion—so-called "illiberal" countries that have the least transparent, weakest, and most corrupt governance systems.

Because it is so difficult to obtain accurate information to allow enforcement, perhaps emission trading should be restricted to advanced industrialized democracies—"liberal" nations. These countries have a common experience with the rule of law; in general, they accept the need for strong international institutions to achieve collective international goals. In addition, these countries also have strong and competent national legal institutions that could be tapped easily to help enforce an international permit system. These countries are part of a "zone of law" where judiciaries are independent, strict rule of law is pervasive, democratic institutions are strong, and governments generally accept strong and intrusive international institutions.[33]

As an interim strategy, restricting trading to the "liberal zone of law" could be useful because it would allow the architects to refine procedures for the system under the most favorable conditions. The system could expand as experience is gained (and as the "zone of law" expands). However, the Kyoto Protocol makes that strategy hard to implement. The protocol's trading system begins in less than a decade (2008)—a mere instant in the evolution of international law. By comparison, it took nearly five decades for the GATT/WTO system to evolve from a relatively simple mechanism that regulated only border tariffs (1948) to one that seriously limited internal nontariff measures (1994). Worse, the Protocol has already prematurely expanded the trading system to illiberal countries that have little experience with, nor interest in, the stable rule of law. The critical suppliers of low-cost permits in the Kyoto framework—Russia and Ukraine—are not part of the "zone of law." In fact, neither is even a member of the WTO, which would be a sign that they were at least capable of preparing their societies to participate in a rule-based international trading system.

As a final strategy, however, restricting trading to a tight "liberal zone of law" makes no sense because the cheapest sites for controlling greenhouse gas emissions are mostly found in countries that are outside the "zone of law"—in Russia, Ukraine, and developing countries. It is no accident that countries where energy is used inefficiently are those where law and markets operate poorly.

In short, none of the conventional approaches to the enforcement problem in international law can solve the problem entirely. Multilateral procedures are generally weak, although not entirely ineffective. Unilateral enforcement is not available in all circumstances. Autonomous enforcement by NGOs and permit holders is unlikely to take hold, except in major cases. These problems would be fewer if nations were to restrict an emission trading system to those countries with strong, independent judiciaries and democratic institutions, but the nations in that "liberal zone of law" are few and tend not to be the sites of low-cost abatement. What can be done?

The difficulty of enforcing international emission trading has an elegant solution: "buyer liability." Making the holders of permits accountable for noncompliance by the countries that issued the permits would build the incentives for compliance directly into the market. It would minimize the need for additional international institutions, with heroic powers, which experience suggests will be both difficult to create and not very effective.

Oddly, many studies, and most conventional wisdom, have advocated "seller liability." The country that originally issued and distributed the permits would be accountable for their compliance; subsequent buyers in other countries would not have their permits devalued if the original issuer defaulted. These studies appear to be motivated by the principal fear that the requirement of tracking the origin and exchange of every permit—which is necessary in a buyer liability system—would raise the transaction costs of the emission trading system.[34] With seller liability, they argue, permit tracking is unnecessary because all permits are mingled in a single world market as a single commodity. In reality, tracking the origin and vintage of every traded emission permit would be very easy; many markets already track much more complicated financial instruments.

Advocates also suggest that seller liability could increase buyer confidence and lead to a less fragmented and more active and efficient market. Having bought from a homogenous world pool of permits, the new permit owner need not worry that his permit could become suddenly worthless if the particular country of origin did not actually implement the emission controls that yielded the permit issued by the originating country.

Seller liability will fail because it is a fiction in international law. The problem with international law is precisely that it cannot efficiently and reliably impose any significant liability on sellers that are most likely to default. Most sellers are likely to be countries where national legal institutions are weakest—they

69

are least likely, on their own, to enforce the integrity of the permit system and most likely to arouse suspicion of cheating. If seller liability is the rule then the game for every devious country will be to stretch the law as far as possible. That stretching point is likely to be quite far because the penalties that can be imposed under international law are cumbersome to apply. Indeed, seller liability encourages sellers to overshoot as wildly as possible—to earn as much as feasible before withdrawal or sanction. Architects of a trading system might try to offset this problem by creating onerous review procedures to approve a country's issuance and sale of permits, but that approach ony partially solves the problem and introduces regulatory uncertainty and other transaction costs that, as in the CDM, will undermine the incentives to trade.

Seller liability eliminates one of the few penalties that is available under international law: expulsion from a treaty. Ejecting a party once it has sold its permits has no effect on the party that has already sold its heritage, and it would merely worsen the twin problems of leakage and permit inflation. Having sold and squandered its earlier allocation, the disgraced country would demand a new supply of permits as compensation to re-enter the system.[35] The most strategic nations probably would cycle inside to outside, inflating the world's permit supply and skimming the surplus as they exit. Thus the chief attraction of seller liability—that a purchaser need not worry about the origin of permits once it has bought them—could easily yield a trading system that unravels quickly when pulled at an open margin.

Because seller liability is a weak incentive for compliance, it would accelerate the need to merge regulations on greenhouse gases with other powerful international institutions—namely, the GATT/WTO trade regime—to deter bogus sellers from defection. That merger is inevitable but will not be easy to arrange. Working it out over the next few years without making major mistakes—after 50 years of development during which the trading regime gave almost no attention to international environmental commitments—is impossible and could severely harm both regimes.[36]

Politically, seller liability invites disaster. It requires that all parties have faith that this novel trillion-dollar international system is working properly. Yet without tracking the origin of every permit, there is no way to unravel the system—and to work out a new burden-sharing agreement—when the emission permit system falters or fails. When Latin American countries defaulted on their debts in the 1980s, the ability to link particular debts and countries was essential to working out a deal—the Brady Plan—that was politically acceptable and allowed all the stakeholders to move on. Americans forget that the United States is the only country with any significant experience using emission trading; the rest of the world has less faith that the markets can work and will gain confidence in the system only if they can track the permits. Yet emission trading with pure seller liability is all or nothing.

Buyer liability makes more sense. Buyers will be located mainly in advanced industrialized countries—the "liberal zone of law" where strong domestic legal institutions are available to ensure that trading rules are followed. National regulators and courts will force buyers to comply, and by doing so they will help assure compliance throughout the trading system.

Certainly buyer liability will impose dreaded transaction costs because prudent buyers will incur the cost of assessing whether the original permit holders will meet their obligations and ensuring that sellers do not overmortgage the reductions in emissions that they are making. But that information is needed in any emission trading system, and it is better to let the market sort it out with the proper incentives than to rely on a universal-membership intergovernmental decision-making body, a UN treaty secretariat, or some other international institution to do the job. Some advocates of seller liability fear that buyer liability exposes buyers to countrywide risks that are difficult for indi-

71

vidual sellers and buyers to control. But that problem is neither novel nor avoidable. Markets for government bonds price country risks every day. And country risk is an important discipline because it dampens the inflationary incentives to oversell and withdraw that could appear in a seller liability system. With buyer liability, governments nearing default on their emission permit stocks would earn lower prices than those where management has been more prudent. Buyer liability enforces compliance through rule-based markets, whereas seller liability requires weak and politicized international institutions to identify and penalize sellers that have not complied.[37]

Other mechanisms can help augment risk pricing, but none is likely to be as efficient and simple as buyer liability. One idea is to use escrow accounts that sellers would forfeit if they did not comply. One-fifth of permit sales, for example, could be put into escrow and released only when compliance is assured. But such accounts raise serious economic and political problems. For escrow accounts to provide a serious deterrent they must be large, but large accounts could squander capital that, improperly invested, could harm the world economy. And just as it has proved politically difficult to alter the investment scheme for the hundreds of billions of public dollars in the United States Social Security Trust Fund, the investment strategy for an international escrow fund—which could easily dwarf the International Monetary Fund (IMF)—would become a political lightning rod. Escrow amounts could be much smaller and more efficient if the amount withheld and forfeited varied with the risk that the seller would default.[38] But that would require differentiating countries based on the expectation of their behavior—elegant in theory but difficult for international legal institutions to implement because major international decisions are often (typically, in international environmental law) determined through a political process that requires unanimous consent. Moreover, the decision that a country should lose all or some of its escrow would be hotly contested; as with enforcement of international legal obli-

MONITORING AND ENFORCEMENT

gations generally, deviants would be able to stretch the law quite far. The result is that escrow accounts are likely to be costly and ineffective in creating the rule of law atmosphere needed for a permit trading system.

Other devices to augment buyer liability are also worth exploring because they could lower the financial implications of enforcement and solve other problems that could appear in a trading system. In particular, it would be useful to couple emission trading with a system of fines (taxes) for noncompliance. Such a scheme would help contain the consequences of noncompliance by giving emitters more confidence that they would be able to comply with their obligations without crippling economic consequences. I return to this issue—linking emission permits and taxes—in the next chapter.

In sum, even if the challenges of allocating permits are overcome, severe problems of monitoring and enforcement are likely to remain. Kyoto has made the problem of monitoring more severe by encompassing the sources and sinks of six greenhouse gases, rather than starting with a focus on what is most important: carbon dioxide from fossil fuels. Emission trading could deftly handle enforcement—one of the most challenging problems of international collective action—but only if buyers are made liable if the permits they hold do not represent true reductions in emissions. Kyoto is silent on whether buyer or seller liability should be the rule, although intense efforts are now under way to develop liability rules. Conventional wisdom appears to be drifting away from logic and towards seller liability. Buyers want to protect their purchases and minimize their worries if, for example, they purchase Russian permits and Russia subsequently defaults on its Kyoto obligations. Sellers, too, seem to favor seller liability. They know that they can command the highest price if buyers need not beware, and that seller liability will not be backed by enforcement sticks that are as powerful as the price signal would be in a buyer liability system. Thus unlike in most areas of commerce—where buyers take heed because they fear being hoodwinked—in this case buyers and sellers alike seem to favor poor accountability. Some permit holders, as well as stakeholders who have the environmental interest at heart, will have the opposite view and favor buyer liability. But their voices may not be strong enough and, so far, have been largely silent. Thus, ironically, in one important area where emission trading could be superior to all other mechanisms for limiting greenhouse emissions, it remains to be seen whether the opportunity will be seized.

CHAPTER 4
Rethinking the Architecture

When viewed in totality, the challenges to building an effective emission trading system are overwhelming. Those difficulties are multiplied by the Kyoto time frame, which requires that nations agree on essentially all the rules that would govern trading no later than approximately 2001. That will allow time for nations to assess and ratify the Protocol and implement the necessary national policies to direct their economies towards compliance by the 2008–2012 budget period.[1] Even 2001 may be too late for some countries.

Technically simple solutions to some of Kyoto's troubles are available, but conventional wisdom and the Kyoto agreement itself prevent them from adoption. For example, restricting Kyoto's emission targets to emissions of CO_2 from the combustion of fossil fuels would ease the problem of monitoring. Few diplomats have considered the severity of the Protocol's monitoring problems, and narrowing the list of gases that the Protocol regulates would require renegotiating the Protocol itself.

Other troubles are fundamental. Paramount is the extreme difficulty of allocating and securing property rights under international law; yet emission trading requires such allocation, and for trading to be efficient the rights must be secure. So far, these troubles have not derailed the Kyoto express—instead, at each impasse diplomats have deferred agreement on solutions to the future. But a diplomatic crisis is brewing as major governments discover that they will not be able to meet Kyoto's emission targets. As that crisis unfolds, should diplomats consider changing course?

This chapter explores alternatives to the Kyoto framework. My focus is on the international architecture for controlling emissions of the gases that cause global warming. I am mindful that governments must not only focus on emissions—as outlined in chapter 1, they must also invest in new knowledge that can lower the cost of controlling emissions in the future, they must adopt policies that increase the ability of societies to adapt to climate changes, and they must explore "geoengineering" schemes that might be needed. But emission control is the central focus of global warming diplomacy, and rightly so. Controlling emissions is the best way to address the most serious consequences of climate change, such as dangers to natural ecosystems and the possibility that a catastrophic change in weather may befall the planet. But what is the best architecture for coordinating international efforts to limit emissions?

I start at the beginning with objectives since the best strategy for controlling emissions depends on what we are trying to achieve. Broadly, the debate over global warming policy has suggested a spectrum of four objectives:

(a) *Do nothing* because the problem is not real
(b) *Defer action* while studying the problem and undertaking policy experiments to explore which emission control efforts are most effective
(c) *Manage multiple risks* that are the consequence of the rising concentration ("stock") of greenhouse gases in the atmosphere

(d) *Avoid a particular threshold* of emissions or concentrations that would cause adverse climate changes.

This chapter will explore which policy instruments best complement these different objectives.

Although all four objectives are logically possible, I dismiss
the first. Reviewing the evidence that climate change is a serious
problem is beyond the scope of this monograph, but the threats
are real and warrant preventive action (see appendix). I focus
on how the threats might be interpreted by the advanced industrialized countries since these nations have the highest emissions, the greatest willingness to devote resources to abatement,
and must take the lead in any serious effort to control emissions.

In general, research has now demonstrated that the most predictable effects of climate change, such as drought and floods
that harm crops and rising sea levels that inundate coastal dwell-
ings, are less worrisome than originally thought. In the advanced
industrialized nations, the fraction of economic activity that is
vulnerable to these impacts is relatively low and the capacity to
adapt is large.[2] In developing countries these predictable effects
are more severe because incomes are lower and the capacity to
adapt is therefore less robust. The poor, who live on slim economic margins, typically are less able to weather a storm than
the wealthy, who can afford more solid foundations.

A sense of justice might compel industrialized countries to
control their emissions so that developing countries are not
harmed. However, justice may not be a sufficiently strong force
if emission control is costly. Moreover, as Thomas Schelling has
argued, even if industrialized countries were centrally worried
about climatic impacts on developing countries, it would be
more efficient to spend resources raising incomes in the developing world and helping economically poor societies to adapt.
These countries already suffer many of the same climatic impacts
that will become more severe in a warmer world—floods in Ban-
gladesh are a serious problem even without raised sea levels.
Helping developing countries to adapt today would be better

than spending money to control emissions that might lessen climatic impacts decades in the future.[3]

Two other dangers of climate change are likely to have a stronger effect on the willingness of industrialized societies to control their emissions. First, changing climate is likely to harm nature, especially unique ecosystems that have adapted to particular local climates. Rapid changes in temperature and humidity could exceed their capacity to adapt and wipe them out. For example, some ecosystems are adapted to mountain cloud forests; they migrate on the slopes as natural changes in the weather alter cloud altitudes. If climate change lifts clouds above the mountaintops entirely, migration will no longer be possible and the ecosystem will disappear.[4] Many such scenarios exist, and though it is impossible to prove their respective likelihood individually, their collective threat to nature might compel action.

Second, and most compelling, is the risk of catastrophe. Growing concentrations of greenhouse gases could cause changes in ocean currents—even the circulation of the entire ocean system. In the past, such changes have occurred naturally and abruptly—wiping out entire species and ecosystems. The accumulation of greenhouse gases could make them more likely. The shift in climate could be much more rapid than the capacity of many natural ecosystems as well as human societies, rich and poor, to adapt.[5] The odds of a catastrophe are probably low, but the effects could be extremely costly. Some catastrophes have been explored but the risks are extremely difficult to assess; other possible catastrophe scenarios may lurk but have not yet been dreamed of by scientists. The risks are real. Moreover, politically, these dangers may resonate especially strongly in advanced industrialized countries, which are able to adapt to many changes but have demonstrated a strong willingness to invest resources to combat overwhelming environmental threats that trounce adaptation.

I begin by analyzing three main alternative architectures to the "cap and trade" system embodied by the Kyoto Protocol, though they also have fatal flaws. Then I advocate a fourth alternative: a hybrid approach that includes elements of each. Finally, I explore some policy measures that will be needed regardless of the particular architecture that is adopted.

Alternative Architectures

When controlling emissions, policy makers must select from a menu of three options. First, they can set targets for the quantity of emissions and leave the market to determine the cost of achieving those targets. That approach leads to the "cap and trade" architecture embodied in the Kyoto Protocol, which I have reviewed already. Second, they can agree on the cost of the effort that each country will make and leave the market to determine what level of emissions results from that effort. That approach typically involves agreeing on the level of taxes that each country would impose, often called simply a "carbon tax" since carbon dioxide is the most important anthropogenic greenhouse gas. Third, governments could agree to intervene directly in the decisions of firms and households and command them to behave differently. In its extreme form this scheme is known as "command and control" and has been a mainstay of environmental policy; here I consider a more flexible version that would allow governments to pick and choose different policies, known as "policies and measures." Table 4.1 summarizes the main pluses and minuses of the different approaches.

Carbon Taxes

One attractive alternative to emission trading would be an international agreement that sets emission prices rather than emission quantities. Some analysts have imagined a global carbon tax levied by a central authority, with revenues collected in an

79

TABLE 4.1

Comparison of Four Architectures for a Greenhouse Gas Regulatory Regime

Instrument	Economic wisdom	Allocation	Monitoring	Enforcement
General approach:				
Cap and Trade (Kyoto)	**Pro:** Best way to empower market forces to control a "threshold" problem, but **Con:** tight quantity limits could force the economy to bear high costs **Con:** Identification and agreement on a dangerous threshold are not imminent	**Con:** Perhaps impossible to negotiate an allocation that would not cause some major emitting nations to withdraw	**Pro:** Easy to monitor permit trades; easy to monitor emissions if trading is restricted to fossil fuel CO_2 only **Con:** Kyoto Protocol includes six greenhouse gases—impossible to monitor all fluxes reliably if trading	**Pro:** Can rely on national legal systems in "liberal" nations if buyer liability is the ru **Con:** If sellers ar liable for noncompliance the system will require internatio enforcement ins tutions of unpre dented strength
Coordinated taxes	**Pro:** Most Efficient instrument when managing a "stock" problem; risks of climate change are mainly a function of the slowly growing "stock" of CO_2 in the atmosphere	**Pro:** Easier to allocate commitments because not distributing semipermanent assets	**Con:** Very difficult to monitor real impact of taxes that are applied to economies in tandem with other tax and investment policies	**Con:** Requires strong and intru sive internation institutions
Coordinated policies	**Pro:** In principle, gives countries the flexibility to determine which efficient policies are best suited to their circumstances **Con:** Invites countries to adopt a hodgepodge of measures that do not sum to an economically rational plan	**Pro:** Flexibility makes it easier to allocate commitments because governments can adopt policies that are easiest to implement through their national political systems	**Con:** Even harder to monitor the real impact of a hodgepodge of policies than for coordinated taxes	**Con:** Requires strong and intru sive internation institutions that pass judgment the way govern ments develop implement national policy politically, an e tremely sensitiv task

TABLE 4.1

…mparison of Four Architectures for a Greenhouse Gas Regulatory Regime *(cont'd)*

…rument	Economic wisdom	Allocation	Monitoring	Enforcement
brid trade …1 tax	**Pro:** Allows countries to regulate multiple risks of climate change mainly as a stock problem; avoids economic shocks caused by forcing compliance with inviolable emission quantity limits	**Pro:** Easier to allocate commitments because countries have greater surety about cost and are more willing to accept more stringent limits	**Pro:** Easy to monitor trades and to monitor emissions (if restricted, initially, to fossil fuel CO_2 only, with provisions to add other fluxes as monitoring improves) **Pro:** Much easier to monitor compliance than in a pure tax approach because the market determines the effective price—intrusive international review mechanisms not needed	**Pro:** Buyer liability would allow most enforcement to occur through legal systems in "liberal" nations **Con:** Undermined if nations adopt "seller liability" rule, or if they expand the system to include a large number of buyers in illiberal nations

international fund, but that design is extremely unlikely since it is nearly impossible to create international institutions that are sufficiently independent and powerful to levy and spend the tax wisely. It is more sensible to imagine an international treaty that would help governments coordinate a series of taxes that each nation would apply. Advocated most prominently by Richard Cooper, a coordinated international carbon tax has three strong advantages.[6]

First, a tax system is likely to be economically more efficient than "cap and trade." A price incentive (e.g., taxes) is better suited to the global warming problem because carbon dioxide, the main cause of global warming, is a "stock" pollutant. The processes that remove carbon dioxide from the atmosphere operate mainly on long time scales (five decades and longer); consequently the concentration of carbon increases slowly in the atmosphere. Thus the benefits from controls on this accumulating stock—less global warming—also rise slowly and steadily. Short-term variations in the exact quantity emitted—over a few years or a decade—do not have much effect on the total stock of carbon dioxide that is accumulating in the atmosphere.

Although the benefits of emission control emerge only gradually, the cost of efforts to limit emissions could be very sensitive to their exact timing. If governments commit to regulating emission quantities but misjudge future costs, they could force early premature retirement of carbon-intensive equipment (e.g., coal-fired power plants)—a waste of resources that could be invested elsewhere in the economy.

Outlined by Weitzman long ago, this basic logic guides when to choose a "price" instrument such as a tax over a "quantities" measure like a cap on emissions.[7] In brief, when the cost of controlling emissions is uncertain but potentially large and the benefits accumulate slowly, it is more efficient for governments to manipulate prices (through taxes) than to cap quantities.[8] The superiority of a price system may be especially great in cases, such as global warming, where the key capital investments are long lived and costly to reverse. Greater certainty of cost makes it easier for firms to plan such investments.[9] Although policy makers often appear to care little about economic efficiency, with tens of billions of dollars at stake in this case efficiency might matter.

Of course, if we had perfect information about the effects of growing carbon dioxide concentrations then we could not treat carbon purely as a "stock" pollutant. Nasty surprises in the climate system might be triggered at particular thresholds of the total concentration and/or rate of change in concentration. If we could identify those thresholds *a priori* then the benefits of managing the carbon stock would no longer rise slowly and uniformly, and it might be worth limiting emission quantities at particular levels to avoid passing nasty thresholds. But we do not have perfect (or even good) information about those thresholds. All we know is that the risk of passing a dangerous threshold grows steadily with the accumulation of greenhouse gases in the atmosphere, and thus the benefits of efforts to control emissions also grow steadily. Even if our goal is to avoid catastrophic climate changes, if we cannot anticipate the concentration that will trigger the catastrophe then it is still appropriate to treat climate change as a stock problem, where the benefits we seek are the result of multiple uncertain effects spread over time.[10]

The second advantage of a tax system is that it could make the allocation of commitments easier politically. The problem of controlling emissions is politically thorny, in part, because the effort could be very costly. When governments set emission quantities they relinquish direct control over the costs. When they set targets a decade or more into the future—as they did in Kyoto—they expose their economies to potentially enormous costs. Wary of worst-case scenarios, in a quantity system governments are likely to be conservative—less willing to make agreements that match the true level of effort that they are willing to undertake. In contrast, setting the tax level allows governments to control costs since the level of effort is approximately proportional to the level of tax. By preventing runaway costs, a carbon tax makes it easier for governments to coordinate ambitious efforts to limit emissions.

A third advantage of a coordinated tax system is that it could eliminate the international financial flows that occur in a trading system, especially when the trading system is first launched and the market equilibrates. A tax system requires governments to price emissions directly—no asset, and therefore no asset flows, need be created. It is true that indirect flows of resources—"leakage"—could result if tax levels differ across countries, but those indirect flows would result from any differential effort to control emissions, whether implemented with taxes or another instrument.

83

An architecture based on coordinated carbon taxes is not without problems, however. Three will be debated; two should not deter efforts to take this idea seriously in international negotiations, but the third is fatal.

First, taxes could be politically difficult to implement because they make the cost of action transparent, and they potentially shift large revenues from emitters to the governments that apply the taxes. Mindful of these facts, politically powerful stakeholders may favor other instruments over taxes. Advocates for environmental protection may favor direct regulation. Even though it is more costly than using market-based approaches such as emission taxes or trading, direct regulation obscures the cost of environmental protection because it exerts direct leverage over polluting activities rather than working through transparent price mechanisms. Nor are major emitters likely to think that a tax approach would best serve their interests. In a tax system they would be liable for the entire cost of the tax. In a tradable permit system with grandfathered permits, major emitters would gain a windfall when permits are allocated that would offset some of the cost of action.

Indeed, the transparency of taxes makes them the "third rail" of environmental policy in some countries. In the United States, notably, any official that advocates the use of a tax instrument risks political electrocution. The lesson learned from the failure of President Clinton's tiny proposed "BTU tax" in 1993 was that Americans will not accept any measure that involves taxes. Whether this conventional wisdom is accurate may be irrelevant—if every American diplomat believes it is true then the tax approach will never be taken seriously in international negotiations. Research that demonstrates that taxes are much superior to "cap and trade" could help change political attitudes, which vary rapidly when compared with the long time frame of the global warming problem.[11] But so far, taxes seem to be off the table for the United States.

In principle, revenue recycling could allow advocates of tax approaches to build a coalition that favors ecological tax reform by exchanging higher taxes on natural resources for a reduction in capital gains and employment taxes. Such reforms could benefit the environment and the economy. So far, however, such ideas are the darling of tax policy engineers but not much evident in practice. Governments have been wary of such reform because it could severely reduce revenues—almost always, when firms are given a strong incentive to control natural resource inputs they find a way, and if inputs decline then revenues from ecological taxes will wither. Clean and green spells poverty for governments that rely on ecological taxation. Taxed firms are often wary of tax reform because they have worked hard to tune the existing tax system to their advantage.

Second, taxes may be objectionable because, in its purest form, the tax instrument would require harmonization at a common tax level. Differential tax levels could lead to leakage; and the transparency of taxes would make it immediately obvious that some nations impose higher carbon costs than others. Governments will be under pressure to ensure that there is a "level playing field" as their firms compete with others. Yet it is unlikely that all nations would accept a measure that is harmonized and identical for each country, unless the measure were so modest—the lowest common denominator—that it required little real change in behavior.

In reality, this second objection is common to all market-based approaches. With the tax instrument, governments that want to stem leakage must equalize prices before launching the tax system. With the cap and trade instrument, the permit market equalizes prices. Politically, this difference may offer an important advantage for the tax instrument over emission permit trading. In a permit system, the only way for a country to exceed the average effort to control emissions would be to accept fewer permits and then watch resources flow overseas as the market equilibrates. In contrast, a coordinated tax approach would let a government implement a more stringent effort without inducing the large flows of assets (permits) that would result as their firms scramble to comply with tight emission caps. Of course, setting carbon prices at levels higher than the average will raise fears of leakage and embolden political opposition among firms that fear competition with firms in other jurisdictions that have lower carbon costs. However, it is easy to overstate the political problems of tilted competition. Firms already tolerate large variations in energy costs across the advanced industrialized nations, and for most industries those differences do not appear to have a large effect on where firms locate their business. That would suggest modest variation in carbon costs (e.g., less than $100 per ton of CO_2) probably would not harm the competitiveness of most energy-using firms.

The third objection, however, may be fatal to the carbon tax approach. Monitoring and enforcement are extremely difficult. In principle, it might be easy to verify whether a country had implemented the agreed tax by simply examining the country's tax code. In practice, it would be extremely difficult to estimate the practical effect of the tax, which is what matters. For example, countries could offset a tax on emissions with less visible compensatory policies that offer loopholes for energy-intensive and export-oriented firms that would be most adversely affected by the new carbon tax. Similarly, governments would implement a carbon tax on top of existing distortions, which would alter the practical effect of the tax. The resulting goulash of prior distortions, new taxes, and political patches could harm the economy and also undermine the goal of making countries internalize the full cost of their greenhouse gas emissions. Indeed, every country that has applied a carbon tax to date has added loopholes—especially for energy-intensive firms—that have blunted the practical effect of the tax on energy prices and behavior.[12]

Even if the marginal effect of the taxes could be measured, and if it were possible to determine that a country was not fulfilling its obligations, the weakness of international law would make enforcement of a tax difficult. If a tax system were restricted to advanced industrialized nations, strong enforcement might not be necessary. Governments in those liberal nations are under pressure from their own electorates to act against global warming, and experience shows that in such situations the fear of being branded a scofflaw has been sufficient to ensure high levels of compliance.[13] However, that hope may not be sufficient if the required tax levels are high or if the system expands to include other countries that are under less severe internal pressure to comply.

The only practical solution to this enforcement problem has already been advocated as the same solution to the compliance and leakage problem in an emission trading system: compliance must be linked with the WTO system. Border tariff adjustments could be used to enforce compliance with the international carbon tax obligations. Importers could raise tariffs against noncompliant countries by an amount equal to the economic advantage gained through noncompliance. Linking the penalty directly (and as swiftly as possible) to the degree of noncompliance would ensure that no economic advantage is gained by countries that are not members of the regulatory effort in good standing while also minimizing the distortion of the WTO to the level that is necessary.

Technically and legally, enforcement of a coordinated tax system through the WTO is not inconceivable. Technically, the task of assessing the proper countervailing tariff would not be trivial, but it is not appreciably different from what nations and international institutions already do when they assess trade effects and determine penalty tariffs. Indeed, governments are already engaged in such activities through the process known as "tariffication"—the translation of various nontariff trade barriers into their equivalent tariff levels. And governments also undertake complex calculations on the trade effects of various policies when they attempt to settle trade disputes. Legally, the famous decision by the WTO on the "shrimp-turtle" dispute has opened the way for governments to use trade measures to enforce compliance with legitimate international environmental objectives.[14]

Although the "shrimp-turtle" decision set a powerful precedent, many hurdles still must be cleared before a scheme for coordinating carbon taxes could rely on border adjustments and trade sanctions to enforce compliance. Developing countries and other advocates of free trade have pilloried the "shrimp-turtle" decision for opening the door to potential abuses in the use of trade sanctions and for allowing rich industrialized nations to use trade sanctions to advance their ecological goals—even if those goals are not universally shared and if sanctions undermine the mission of free trade. Nor is it clear exactly how to graft a system for enforcing carbon controls on to the existing WTO institutions. In particular, the WTO enforcement system relies on formal disputes that are mainly bilateral in character—one WTO member sues when it is hurt by the actions of another WTO member. That bilateral system works well in trade because trade is mainly a bilateral activity. For global warming and other global environmental problems, however, the effects of noncompliance are diffused across all compliant nations and thus the incentive for any individual state to take action is diffused. It may be more efficient to create a compliance mechanism that is more automatic and multilateral, rather than relying on individual states to initiate and shepherd cumbersome disputes.

In principle, the foundation for a multilateral compliance mechanism already exists in the WTO's Trade Policy Review Mechanism (TPRM), which undertakes regular multilateral reviews of trade policies. The current mandate of the TPRM could be expanded to include assessment of whether countries have implemented the required carbon taxes; the TPRM could also provide other services, such as issuance of warnings and calculation of countervailing tariffs, which would be necessary to make enforcement work efficiently. But these ideas, for now, are hypothetical, and the political difficulty of creating them should not be underestimated. What is needed is an international institution that can pass judgment on whether national policies conform with international standards—a politically delicate task that is feasible only once parties are confident that the international mechanism can work impartially. Confidence building took several decades for the GATT and WTO system. Even now, members are wary of creating strong institutions. The TPRM's mandate explicitly prohibits it from passing judgment on a nation's trade policy or initiating disputes that would enforce compliance with WTO's agreements—rather, its purpose is to promote learning and awareness.[15]

In sum, it is conceivable that nations could coordinate carbon taxes if the taxes were sufficiently low that monitoring and enforcement were not significant issues. Several studies suggest that the optimal tax might, indeed, be very low—perhaps $10 per ton of CO_2; the problem, however, is that it may be infeasible, for the foreseeable future, to invent the institutions necessary for monitoring and enforcing a more stringent tax.

Coordinated Policies and Measures

Many discussions of environmental policy focus on the choice between "markets" and "command and control" policy instruments. We have already evaluated the two leading contenders for a market-based approach: trading and taxing. Here we evaluate the command and control alternative. As with "markets," there is no single type of "command and control." Moreover, the terminology of "command and control"—invented by advocates of market-based instruments—conjures images of Stalinist regulation that is infeasible at the international level. Quite apart from the severe inefficiencies of "command and control" approaches, it is politically impossible to create a centralized international authority that would dictate technologies and policies for nations and firms to adopt.

Thus here I explore the only realistic option for an international policy instrument that is consistent with traditional "command and control" regulatory approaches. The option is to coordinate "policies and measures." Unlike Cooper's harmonized carbon tax, international coordination of policies and measures would not require the imposition of an identical policy instrument in all countries. Instead, in principle countries could pick and choose what best suits their local circumstances—some might adopt price instruments, others could impose emission caps, and still other countries would resort to technology standards, voluntary agreements, or sundry other instruments.

In principle, this approach is attractive not only because it is flexible but also because policy coordination would force governments to focus on what they (and firms on their territory) might *do* to control emissions. Focusing on action would help to break the odd stasis on global warming policy: the political process has been an oasis for goal setters yet a desert of action. At the 1988 Toronto Conference many nations and politicians proclaimed the goal of cutting carbon dioxide emissions 20% below 1988 levels by the year 2005[16]—yet no major nation seriously attempted to meet the Toronto goal, though most industrialized nations professed that the "Toronto target" was a centerpiece of their global warming policy and a few still do. The Kyoto process repeated the experience, with more modest goals and stretched timetables.

A system of coordinated policies would consist of national policy plans developed through a process of mutual scrutiny and negotiation. Each country would propose a package of actions; others would scrutinize and adjust their own proposals accordingly. The collective effort would emerge through negotiations focused on each nation's proposed actions, rather than through aggregation of emission targets invented by diplomats and not based on any viable plan for implementation. In the negotiations leading to the 1997 Kyoto Protocol the European Union argued that the protocol should be organized around a menu of policies and measures (known by their acronym PAMs); governments would be required to adopt all those on a common list and to choose among others on separate à la carte lists. Each country would determine on its own how best to contribute to the collective effort; somehow, progress toward individual and collective goals would be measured with quantitative emission targets. The Europeans never clearly articulated how this system would work, and skeptics saw it as a ploy by the European Commission to make it easier for bureaucrats to intervene in economies and impose their favorite carbon-cutting solutions, such as efficiency standards and subsidies for windmills and other zero-carbon renewable energy sources. The only vestige of the politically stillborn proposal is Annex A of the protocol, which includes a broad list of policies and measures that governments might adopt.

Longtime observers of the scene will recognize that this proposal has much in common with the concept of "pledge and review," which was among the proposals discussed in 1991 when the Framework Convention on Climate Change was in the initial stages of design. The vision, though never elaborated in detail, would entail countries pledging packages of policies to address global warming; subsequent review would check whether commitments were being honored and identify needed adjustment. Many pressure groups and countries that professed to favor effective regulation of greenhouse gases opposed "pledge and review"; they feared that pledges would be broken and review would be whitewash. Hence "pledge and review" quickly perished and binding targets and timetables were embraced as the only way to make governments stick to their commitments. Sadly, little attention was given to working out a more detailed vision for pledge and review and the episode became one of the many wrong turns in the short history of efforts to develop a collective response to global warming. The European PAMs proposal prior to Kyoto made no intellectual advance on the basic idea of pledge and review that had been worked out six years earlier.

In principle, the policies and measures approach has many advantages. With it, unlike cap and trade and coordinated taxes, countries would have liberal flexibility to determine how they would contribute to the collective goal of managing emissions. That extra flexibility might make it relatively easy for governments to agree on an initial allocation of effort. Because the costs and efficacy of different policies and measures is difficult to measure, the exact distributional consequences of an initial agreement may be unclear. Indeed, some scholars have suggested that such opacity could actually ease the process of reaching agreement—since the exact consequences of any particular package of policies and measures would be unclear, governments might be inclined to focus only on the rough allocation of effort; strategic quibbling about the details would largely disappear.[17] Moreover, the approach would share a positive attribute of emission taxes in requiring only that governments move their economies in the right direction, rather than comply with strict, binding emission targets.

Among the models for policy coordination is the Marshall Plan, advocated by Thomas Schelling.[18] Part of the plan's success was due to a system of mutual peer review that forced recipient governments to explain what they would do with their Marshall Plan aid. Governments proposed a package of measures and costs; through peer review they arrived at an allocation of the aid and a sound plan for how to spend it efficiently. Today, the Organization for Economic Cooperation and Development (OECD), which grew out of the Marshall Plan, effectively runs mutual peer review in science and technology policy, economic policy, and several other areas of industrial policy. The Marshall Plan and OECD experiences have shown that mutual review helps focus attention on policies that work; it also helps build the shared experience and institutions that make it possible to assess whether promised actions will have the intended effects. Nonbinding performance benchmarks could help ensure that all countries are working, more or less, towards sensible common goals.

Other partial models for a system of coordinated policies include the General Agreement on Tariffs and Trade (GATT),[19] which has reduced trade barriers through eight "rounds" of negotiations. Each round has become increasingly complex (and required longer to complete), resulting in ever-larger package deals. Unlike the Kyoto Protocol, which was negotiated mostly during a few hurried months late in 1997, the package deals have focused on complex actions and countries' plans for implementation, rather than simple targets and hopes that implementation will follow. Early rounds, which focused on tariffs, were relatively easy to complete, implement, and enforce; more recent rounds have tried to regulate myriad nontariff barriers to trade, which have been more difficult to assess and codify into enforceable agreements.[20] In the case of climate change, a similar evolution might occur. Early rounds would focus on building institutions and undertaking relatively simple actions. Later rounds would deepen cooperation and strengthen institutional capacity, making it possible to address more complex and difficult problems of policy coordination. The commitments, political pressure to act, and institutions could coevolve. In contrast, even a rudimentary cap and trade or harmonized tax system requires elaborate institutional capabilities before it can begin operation—the cap and trade system requires a scheme for allocating permits, and the tax system requires the capacity to measure the impact of the tax.

The flexibility of the policies and measures approach would make it possible to follow the advice of Robert Hahn and treat the early international efforts to slow global warming as a series of policy experiments. Countries could select from a variety of mechanisms—cap and trade, taxes, command and control, and voluntary agreements—and an extensive process of documentation and review could facilitate assessment of which are most effective and efficient.[21] This approach could also force governments to assess, from the earliest stages, the complementarities and conflicts between policy instruments since it is unlikely that any government's stringent effort to control greenhouse gases would rely on a single instrument. For example, governments that wanted to use taxation to control emissions of CO_2 from combustion of fossil fuels would need to select another instrument for the greenhouse gas fluxes that are less easy to monitor. With the policies and measures approach they could coordinate the tax level on CO_2 while also coordinating complementary measures—such as standards for the timing of flooding and fertilizer applications in rice paddies—to ensure that the other greenhouse gas fluxes did not escape control.[22]

However, the policies and measures approach has two fatal flaws that make it unusable as the central framework for significant coordinated efforts to control emissions. First, it is the most difficult to monitor and verify of the major options considered in this chapter. As with the carbon tax approach, governments would need to vest institutions with the capacity to verify that each country is doing its share of the collective effort. However, accurately measuring the impacts of government policies would be even more difficult in this case because many "policies and measures" will not be associated with any particular price and thus will be difficult for economists to model. Indeed, one of the great political attractions of this approach is that its economic impacts are so difficult to identify.

Second, because the policies and measures approach is not a single instrument but, rather, a broad umbrella, it encourages governments to implement piecemeal instruments that are more complex, less transparent, and less efficient than a single market-based instrument. The dangers are already evident in the European Union, which proposed the idea of policies and measures. To control transportation emissions the EU is sponsoring a large technology program to improve the efficiency of new aircraft engines, and it has negotiated voluntary agreements with automobile manufacturers to raise the efficiency of new automobiles.

In tandem, some European countries are applying carbon taxes to parts of their economy, while others have initiated emission trading programs. A hodgepodge of voluntary and mandatory efficiency standards for appliances and other energy-using equipment, developed in Brussels as well as in the individual countries, is also in the works.[23] The voluntary agreements are especially problematic since they are based on the loose promise that voluntary action will forestall additional binding regulation later on, which leaves regulators with few options if they discover that their packages of measures do not add up. Only if regulators were omniscient could they devise a package of piecemeal measures that regulate behavior along lines of equal marginal cost and thus lowest total cost. Because the impact of policy on long-term emissions would be especially difficult to quantify, governments would be inclined to compare the cost of their efforts, but that would only worsen the problem. Countries with liberal subsidies and inefficient energy standards programs would appear to be doing the most even though their vast expenditure may have relatively little impact on emissions. The process would reward expenditure rather than efficiency.

These problems could be reduced if governments were to negotiate performance benchmarks along with their packages of policies and measures. Benchmarks, such as total or sector emission levels, could focus governments on the effectiveness of policies and also make it easier for other governments to verify that agreed efforts were being implemented. If actual performance deviates from the benchmark, peer review could focus on why— separating unanticipated effects from overt failures to comply. A useful precedent is OECD's system of Environmental Performance Reviews, which adopts a country's own environmental protection goals as benchmarks for reviewing performance. Similarly, the Marshall Plan process included extensive peer review, focused on individual and collective performance standards.

Thus the policies and measures approach is perhaps useful as a general framework for *starting* the process of international

95

cooperation on climate change. Unlike full-blown emission trading or coordination of carbon taxes, a modest policies and measures approach would be relatively easy to establish and would focus attention on actions rather than hopeful emission targets. And the policies and measures approach offers a framework within which governments can experiment with alternative policy instruments; in particular, this framework would allow governments to use market-based instruments for the easily monitored emissions (fossil fuel CO_2) while simultaneously coordinating policies for the other gases that are more difficult to monitor.

However, this approach will be useful *only* if governments support it by creating serious institutions that evaluate performance, promote learning, and help ensure that the myriad of adopted policies makes sense as a rational whole. The Marshall Plan experience shows that it is possible to devise a system that performs these review, allocation, and verification functions reasonably well. The WTO experience shows that it is possible to assemble complex policies into package deals that are broadly coherent. But the Marshall Plan and WTO experiences also indicate the difficulties with monitoring and enforcement. Enforcement under the Marshall Plan would have been nearly impossible without the enormous carrot of American aid. And, as discussed earlier, the WTO enforcement system is cumbersome because it operates on a case-by-case basis; the TPRM, which could offer more systematic oversight of trade policies, is explicitly not intended for verification and enforcement.

Thus I doubt that the policies and measures approach will be viable as a permanent strategy for dealing with global warming. It is akin to making a meal of sampling hors d'oeuvres—tantalizing in its convenience and variability yet ultimately not robust. As governments plan more stringent and costly action to control emissions they will need to shift towards the central use of a market-based instrument and away from the hodgepodge encouraged by the policies and measures approach.

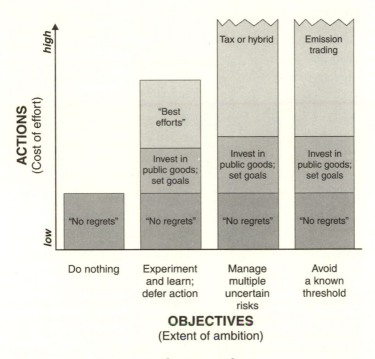

FIGURE 4.1: Objectives and actions

Comparing the Alternatives

Thus we have examined three broad alternative architectures for slowing the accumulations of greenhouse gases in the atmosphere: (1) emission caps and trading, (2) emission taxes, and (3) policies and measures. And, as mentioned in chapter 1, regardless of which alternative they choose, policy makers should also invest in the public good of basic research, and in other activities such as geoengineering and setting long- and short-term goals.

How do these strategies correspond with the four potential objectives of climate policy outlined earlier? Figure 4.1 suggests an answer. If the objective is to do nothing because global warming poses no threats (column 1) then the best strategy is either inaction or the creation of a system for coordinating policies and measures, which in essence would help countries identify and implement policies that cost nothing yet control emissions—so-called "no regrets" policies. (Often these policies, such as information programs, require expenditure by government and thus are not viewed as completely costless—even though they are beneficial for society as a whole.) This strategy does not lock in any particular approach; there is not much need for monitoring or enforcement because the stakes are low and action would correspond with the party's own self-interest.

At the other extreme, if the objective is to limit the build-up of greenhouse gases to a particular threshold (column 4) then trading is the best approach. Only with trading is it possible to ensure that agreed emission caps are honored. The allocation problem is severe, but if the world knew that it were collectively facing a catastrophe that would occur at a particular threshold then it might be possible to conclude the omnibus allocation needed to distribute the permits. Some nations and most environmental NGOs already believe that the world is facing that situation, but so far their influence has been mainly in setting ambitious goals rather than real targets and permit allocations. The governments include the low-lying island nations—for whom even modest sea level rise could be catastrophic—but they have little power in world affairs.

Governments in most of the advanced industrialized countries view the climate problem as somewhere in the middle (column 2 or 3). Their publics are increasingly convinced that the dangers of climate change are real, but there is no agreement on the severity of the risk. Governments are under pressure to implement policies that extend beyond "no regrets," but there is no agreement on a particular threshold that must be avoided; nor does it appear likely that policy makers will be able to identify a particular threshold. Rather, the goal is to reduce and manage risks caused by the accumulating "stock" of greenhouse gases. There is growing interest in reducing (or even eliminating) carbon dioxide emissions from the energy system over the long term—a process known as decarbonization. For the last century decarbonization of the world energy system has proceeded at a leisurely 0.3% per year as coal has been supplanted by less carbon-intensive oil as the top energy source and, now, gas is overtaking oil. Additional policies, such as eliminating subsidies for coal production and taxing carbon emissions, could accelerate decarbonization.[24] Experts are intrigued by the possibility that they could accelerate decarbonization within the normal turnover of the capital stock and not impose much (or any) additional cost on the economy, and such scenarios add to mounting pressure on governments to implement carbon policy. Governments have an idea of the costs that their societies are willing to tolerate, but they do not know what meeting particular emission targets will cost nor exactly what level of carbon control is best.

For problems with these characteristics, the best strategy depends on the perception of the severity of the problem. For stakeholders that are still wary of any costly action the best strategy is to adopt a policies and measures system under which they can make their "best effort" to control emissions—to undertake a variety of policies and measures, to learn from different efforts, and not to worry much about the allocation of effort because the stakes are low (column 2). In essence, this approach defers more stringent action to the future when more is known about the problem at hand and the cost of action may be lower as efforts to invest in public goods bear fruit. For stakeholders more convinced that the problem warrants more stringent action, the ideal strategy is coordinated taxes (column 3).

There is no robust way to declare whether column 2 or 3 is the better approach. The answer depends on one's assessment of the literature on the risks of climate change and one's willingness to take risks with the planet and economy. It also depends on whether one thinks that governments could make efficient investments in basic research that will dramatically lower the cost of controlling emissions in the future—or if new low-cost strategies for limiting (or eliminating) emissions of greenhouse gases will appear autonomously. Some studies suggest that carefully designed policies to shift technologies could achieve rapid decarbonization at little or no cost.[25] And it is widely agreed that technological innovation is centrally important to improving the energy system.[26] But the history of overt policy efforts to alter technological trajectories is checkered with disaster.[27] It is especially unlikely that a strategy that focuses on (or hopes for) technological innovation would be effective unless there were at least modest efforts to impose a price on emissions of greenhouse gases. Technology investments, especially by the public sector, are often wasteful unless guided by prices and private market-oriented investment decisions. Private firms will participate if they believe that future emission controls are likely, and the only way that governments can credibly signal future action is by implementing at least some modest policies today. Especially when operating within the framework of international law—within which governments can defect from inconvenient commitments—mere statements of intention are not credible signs of action. For these reasons, the best way to send credible signals is to demonstrate real action—to implement even a small tax and thus signal that a stiffer price could follow in the future. In sum, my assessment is that the best strategy lies in column 3. If, in the future, particular thresholds are identified we need the capacity to shift to a strategy in column 4.

But none of the architectures discussed can deliver success in column 3. A system of "policies and measures" could help coordinate actions by governments, but such a system is prone to inefficiency and extremely difficult to monitor and enforce. That is why it is suited only for modest, low-cost, and self-enforcing international commitments, such as implementing "no regrets" policies. Yet column 3 envisions going beyond "no regrets." Best suited, in theory, for column 3 is a system of internationally coordinated emission taxes. But monitoring and enforcement of a coordinated tax system would be extremely difficult. As with the "policies and measures" approach, strict monitoring and enforcement might not be necessary if tax levels were low and incentives to cheat were weak. But it makes little sense to build an elaborate architecture that would be ineffective if nations ever wanted to implement more stringent emission control efforts by increasing the tax levels. Finally, nations could greatly ease the enforcement problems with these other strategies by adopting an architecture based on emission trading and buyer liability. If they restricted that system to emissions of carbon dioxide from the combustion of fossil fuels then monitoring would be feasible as well. But emission trading runs into trouble when nations attempt to allocate permits in the first place. In principle they could use emission trading for the objectives in column 3 by adjusting the number of permits in circulation and thus adjusting the emission levels as scientific information and political concern about the risks of climate change evolve. And, in principle, a trading system could make it easy to cap emissions at a certain level if nations wanted to avoid a dangerous threshold—column 4. But allocation and cold starting the system remain high hurdles.

Must we choose among second-best strategies—each of which falls severely short or, worse, will be stillborn?

A Hybrid Approach

A fourth architecture is also feasible. It would combine elements from each of the three architectures already evaluated—"policies and measures," emission trading, and taxation.

The core of this approach would be a hybrid of emission trading and taxation. The approach would not force the architects of a global warming treaty to choose between caps on emission quantities or coordinating emission taxes. Instead, govern-

101

ments would set targets for emission quantities and also for prices.

Governments would set targets for emission quantities and create an emission trading system. At the same time, they would also agree on a maximum price for the tradable permits. Any government that participates in the system could issue and sell new emission permits at the agreed price. If the trading price rises above the target price then firms could purchase new permits from governments at the target price. If the trading price dips below the target price then firms could simply purchase less costly permits on the open market. In effect, the target price would cap the cost of acquiring permits and thus also give firms greater surety about the cost of compliance.[28]

In a properly designed hybrid system the target price would not be set at an extremely high level that would kick in only as a "last resort" mechanism in case the cost of compliance was extremely high. The U.S. sulfur dioxide trading program includes an escape mechanism that operates in that manner—the escape price, which takes the form of a fine, is nearly ten times today's trading price for sulfur dioxide permits, with the result that the escape mechanism is never used. Rather, the target price should be set and adjusted to the level that nations agree will define their joint effort. At the same time, the quantity of permits allocated should also equal the expected quantity of emissions from that joint effort. Such an approach would force governments to be transparent about the combination of prices and quantities that will result from their ambitions to limit emissions.

How well does such a hybrid system survive the three critical tests that I have applied to the other architectures—allocation, monitoring, and enforcement? In answering that question I make several interrelated arguments. Under the hybrid system it is much easier to allocate commitments and permits, which is the central problem that makes a pure textbook emission trading system infeasible. Moreover, in contrast with a pure textbook system of coordinated emission taxes, it is easier to monitor compliance of governments with their commitments under the hybrid system. Finally, it should be relatively easy to enforce compliance through "buyer liability." Now I elaborate the arguments in more detail.

Compared with textbook emission trading, governments will find it much easier to allocate commitments under the hybrid system. The cap on permit prices would allow governments and firms to contain the cost of complying with the protocol. That would ease allocation for four reasons. First, governments could afford to be less risk averse when allocating permits because their diplomats could confidently reject the worst-case scenarios in which abatement costs are much higher than expected. That would not only ease negotiation of a treaty that allocates commitments but also facilitate ratification afterward. Some of Kyoto's troubles in the United States stem from the fact that American emissions have grown steadily since Kyoto and policies to limit emissions have been delayed, which has multiplied the costs of compliance and raised the specter of even higher possible compliance costs.

Second, surety about cost will make it easier to launch an international regulatory system that includes many novel components. For example, a key factor in the cost of complying with the Kyoto Protocol is the efficiency of the Clean Development Mechanism (CDM). The CDM is essential to the Kyoto treaty—and to any successor to Kyoto—because it is a way to engage developing countries and perhaps also to achieve low-cost abatement of greenhouse gases. Yet nothing like the CDM has been attempted under international law, and it is proving difficult to agree on the rules that will govern how countries can use the CDM to earn emission credits. In practice, the extent to which the CDM actually reduces compliance costs will depend on many factors that are difficult to anticipate—for example, the efficiency of the process for approving CDM projects.[29] Without a mechanism for containing costs, governments will be reluctant to adopt stringent commitments that envision the serious use of such novel mechanisms. That reluctance will make it unlikely that novel mechanisms will be exercised much, making it hard for the mechanisms to evolve and improve through learning.[30]

Third, greater surety about cost will make it easier for governments to negotiate an allocation that corresponds with their marginal cost of abatement. Achieving this would mean that the system would already be near equilibrium; international flows would be small when trading begins. Economically, the large international flows of finance and permits that could occur during equilibration of a trading system may not matter. Politically, however, they are very problematic. Part of the controversy about the surplus that Russia and Ukraine obtained under the Kyoto Protocol exists because shipping vast financial resources to Russia and Ukraine is not politically popular.[31]

Fourth, the hybrid system may make it easier to expand participation in the regulatory system over time. If target prices are low enough then governments will actually print and sell additional permits, which will limit the value of the existing property rights. Such agreed and automatic procedures for printing new permits can ensure, at least partially, that the permits do not acquire characteristics of a secure property right. And, to the extent that the system is not built on secured property rights it will be easier for the participants to adjust and reallocate burdens over time, which is necessary if they want to alter participation in the scheme. To the extent that governments actually print and sell additional permits, the hybrid system becomes more like a collective effort to coordinate prices—and thus allocation and adjustment of participation should become much easier than in a textbook system of tradable property rights.

More analysis is needed to explore the extent to which diplomats would, in practice, actually find it easier to adjust participation in the hybrid system than under textbook trading. The answers are important. Once any free trading system equilibrates then the marginal cost of emitting greenhouse gases in each participating economy will be identical.[32] But preferences for spending resources on slowing global warming vary—for example, West European nations are keenly concerned about climate change, but most Russians care little (or would even welcome warmth). With such diverse preferences, it is unlikely that all countries would agree to stay within a regime that, once it has equilibrated, would require each member to sustain identical price signals and thus identical levels of effort.[33] These problems suggest that it would be wiser to restrict any permit trading system, including the hybrid architecture explored here, to countries that demonstrate similar willingness to impose costs on emissions. Moreover, as discussed in chapter 2, evidence from cooperation on other complex problems suggests that it is much easier to build sophisticated international institutions when participants are few. If the hybrid approach, in contrast with textbook emission trading, makes reallocation easier then it would also make it politically much easier to start with a limited number of like-minded participants and let the system expand as the institutions mature.

As with a textbook trading system, it should be relatively easy to monitor compliance under the hybrid architecture. Monitoring is especially needed in two areas. First, emission monitoring is needed to ensure that actual emissions do not exceed the number of permits in each government's account. (Here, as elsewhere, I speak of government-owned permits because governments, as agents of nations, would have the obligation under international law to balance their books. Below I explore the impact of the hybrid approach on how governments might allocate permits within nations.) If the architects restrict this system to fossil fuel emissions of CO_2 then emission monitoring will be relatively easy.

Second, monitoring is needed on government sales of additional permits. A government that sells below the agreed price would reap all the revenue from the extra sales and also cause

105

excessive emissions; procedures are needed to spot this out-come. In a textbook tax system, such monitoring is difficult be-cause there could be a large difference between the nominal tax level (which is easy to monitor by looking at a country's tax code) and the effective tax level (which is what matters). In the hybrid system that difference disappears because the permit market governs the price; if that market is efficient then the price will mirror the actual cost of emissions. Monitoring requires looking only at the trading price of permits, which is an easy task. If each permit is marked with its origin then it will be rela-tively easy to trace underpriced new permits back to the guilty seller and to correct the bias with an additional tax.

Finally, enforcement in a hybrid system could rely mainly on buyer liability. As with textbook emission trading, buyers would be accountable if the seller defaulted. The system would create private incentives for good monitoring—as in other financial markets—and it would align the price of permits with risks of default.

In brief, the hybrid system offers the advantages of both the quantity and price systems and greatly reduces the most trou-bling disadvantages of each.[34] I close by tying three loose ends. First, my vision for the hybrid approach is, so far, silent about the fluxes of greenhouse gases other than fossil fuel CO_2. The other fluxes are still too hard to measure at the level of whole nations and thus inappropriate for high-stakes international treaties and financial instruments where accurate measurement is important. One remedy for this problem is to coordinate "poli-cies and measures" for the other gases. Many useful programs are already under way to implement low-cost and "no regrets" policies to reduce these gases—for example, programs to capture and use methane from landfills and to plug leaky natural gas pipelines. The international architecture should provide for co-ordination of these policies, even as the central system focuses on fossil fuel CO_2. The other remedy is to award tradable credits for actions that control these fluxes on a project-by-project basis in cases where governments can monitor the fluxes accurately. Project-by-project approaches—such as the CDM and JI in the Kyoto Protocol—are cumbersome, as I have already discussed in chapter 2. But they can be effective mechanisms when an abatement project offers strong economic advantages; the CDM concept is especially important because it is a way to engage countries that otherwise would undertake no abatement effort. Moreover, allowing project-by-project credits would also create economic incentive to improve monitoring of these fluxes.

A second loose end is that I have said nothing about how nations might implement the hybrid strategy. In a textbook emission trading system, governments have no choice but to adopt a domestic emission trading system if they want to be sure that they will comply with binding emission caps.[35] This hybrid strategy relaxes that requirement because it tolerates emission levels that deviate from the quantity targets. In principle, governments could adopt rules that would allow countries to implement their obligations under the hybrid system entirely with emission taxes. Countries that chose that option might be required to undergo more thorough review so that differences between the nominal and effective tax rate could be spotted. Other countries might choose to implement their obligations with a pure emission trading system, although I doubt that many would make that choice if other governments were implementing the hybrid approach—if the price of permits ever rose above the target then all the revenue from the extra permit sales would flow offshore. So, in practice, even the hybrid approach would constrain how governments implemented their international obligations. Indeed, it seems likely that any serious concerted effort to control emissions of greenhouse gases will require a significant intrusion into how governments implement policies for the activities that cause emissions of greenhouse gases. Since most aspects of modern industrial economies emit greenhouse gases, serious greenhouse gas control will transform the intrusiveness of international environmental law. For some observers that may appear to be a radical and dangerous inflection point.[36] But in other areas of international law the advanced industrialized nations are already passing this point. In trade, the World Trade Organization constrains national policies on food safety, governmental procurement, taxation, and many other areas that previously were viewed as securely within the domain of national policy. In arms control, treaties aspire to regulate private activities that might conceal or promote illicit arms production—chemical manufacturing that cloaks poison gas production, for example.

A third loose end is that the hybrid system may appear complicated and more cumbersome than the seductively simple cap and trade architecture of the Kyoto Protocol. But a close look suggests not. As efforts to implement the Kyoto Protocol advance it is becoming clear that creating and managing a textbook emission trading system is complicated. [Adding JI and CDM to that textbook system—to create what I have called full-blown (i.e., worldwide) trading—multiplies the complexity.] Indeed, the hybrid system requires that governments negotiate still more elements than under a textbook trading system—notably, it requires that governments set the target price, in addition to target qualities. But this extra step merely requires that diplomats be transparent about the expected economic consequences of their efforts to control emissions. No responsible government would negotiate a cap on quantities without also analyzing the expected effect on prices. Adopting an architecture that would promote more price transparency would not raise the complexity. It would help focus a reasoned debate and yield more realistic international commitments. Kyoto's troubles stem, in large part, from ambitious claims for the control of emission quantities and scant attention to prices and economic consequences.

CHAPTER 5
After Kyoto: What Next?

It is perhaps most important for governments and pressure groups to ensure that, when the Kyoto Protocol fails, the public learns that the failure was due, in large part, to the mechanisms chosen. The problems with Kyoto are not merely a matter of mustering the "political will" to swallow a bitter pill. Rather, Kyoto's troubles originate with its architecture—strict emission targets and trading—which is especially ill suited to the fact that the level of emissions for the most important greenhouse gases is inherently unpredictable. Policy makers cannot credibly set targets; international law is a poor mechanism for allocating permits and controlling a permit market with trillions of dollars at stake. And the Protocol's strict short-term targets give the appearance of serious action but belie the reality that no major government has a viable plan for compliance. Less than a decade remains before 2008—not enough time for Western nations to plan and implement cost-effective investments that would be needed if they were to comply with the Kyoto targets entirely through action within their borders. Compliance would be easier to acheive if governments were to cold start an international emission trading system based on the Kyoto Protocol, but doing that would result in huge Western purchases of excess permits from Russia and Ukraine. Few legislatures will consent to sending perhaps one hundred billion dollars Eastward. A full-blown trading system could also make it easier for the West to comply with Kyoto's targets by making it possible to earn credits from investments that reduce emissions in developing countries. But there are still no rules to govern the crediting of those investments and the lead times are at least several years long. Time has run out on the Kyoto Protocol.

A sensible strategy for moving forward would have three elements.

The first step out of this mess requires reopening the Kyoto deal. Solving the problem of the excess allocation to Russia and Ukraine requires giving less generous targets to these countries, which cannot be done without renegotiating the schedule of commitments that is the core of the Kyoto Protocol. That problem cannot be ignored because the Russian and Ukrainian windfall will be a political showstopper for ratification in the United States and is the main root of European objections to emission trading. Solving this problem is also essential if the treaty is to make its full promised contribution towards solving the environmental problem at hand. As it presently stands, nations could comply fully with the Kyoto pact, enrich Russian and Ukrainian oligarchs, and yet do practically nothing to slow global warming. The IIASA/WEC "middle course" scenario shown in figure 2.1 suggests that the windfall for the reforming nations is nearly as large as the projected deficit in the West. This windfall is thus a double political liability—an obscene wealth transfer to Russia and Ukraine, and one that greatly eases compliance but does not result in lower global emissions.

The Kyoto pact must also be reopened to grapple with the problems posed by the multiple gases that cause global warming and to create incentives to improve monitoring. One solution to the monitoring problem is to distinguish among sources and sinks according to the ability to monitor fluxes accurately. Only well-monitored fluxes would be included in the core regulatory system, such as emission trading or other highly quantified commitments. Another solution is to discount gases and projects according to the uncertainty in their emission estimates.[1] Both approaches would give an incentive to improve monitoring—in the former, improved data quality would make it possible to earn additional credits in the core regulatory system, and in the latter better data would reduce the penalty for investing in abatement projects that yield uncertain reductions in emissions. But both solutions require amending the political and legal agreement that was accepted in Kyoto. A step-by-step approach would require augmenting the Kyoto targets, which currently apply to a single basket of gases, with additional targets for individual fluxes, gases, or baskets of gases. A step-by-step approach would also require new rules to regulate emissions of the gases that are excluded from the trading system so that poor measurement does not become an excuse for inaction. The discounting approach would require political decisions on the level and mode of discounting, which could alter the stringency of the emission targets and the cost of compliance. None of these "technical" solutions can be implemented without high-level political decisions that are akin to renegotiating the core obligations of the Protocol.

Second, any agreement to slow global warming will require strong and capable international institutions. Already it is clear that governments are wary of developing international institutions that would be necessary to oversee the commitments made in Kyoto. Even more capable institutions would be needed to oversee the broader and deeper commitments required for a more serious effort to limit climate change. Particularly urgent is the need for institutions that can gather and assess the information necessary both to assess compliance after the fact and to inform future negotiations on allocating burdens.

111

So far the effort to slow global warming has been one of the most effective environmental treaties in getting countries to report data, especially emission estimates. But little of the data is actually useful. Reports are incomplete and lack the uniformity necessary to make them comparable.[2] The data reported make it possible to tabulate national emissions, but the common framework that has been developed for emissions accounting is largely optional, and most countries' own accounting methods are neither transparent nor comparable with the methods used in other nations. The reporting framework provides almost no basis for analyzing uncertainties and biases in emission estimates. Even worse are data on policies that countries are implementing and planning, which are essential to assessing, *ex ante*, which countries are on track to meet their obligations, the share of the collective burden that each nation is shouldering, and whether commitments must be renegotiated and reallocated. Only skeletal international capacity exists to analyze reported data, and major governments seem content to keep that capacity weak. The FCCC has created a system of in-depth reviews that are conducted by independent experts. It is a first step in improving the utility of the data that countries report, but the road will be long. The reviews include in-country visits that last only a few days yet cover, in essence, each nation's entire economy. No developing country has ever undergone a review; rather, reviewers focus on the industrialized nations where transparency already reigns.[3] The mandate is to be "facilitative, non-confrontational, open and transparent"; the review teams engage more in confidence building and aiding the "host country" to mobilize resources, rather than in detailed scrutiny and criticism.[4] Whereas Rabkin (1998) has cautioned against the Kyoto Protocol because it empowers unelected bureaucrats to make decisions that affect national liberties, the real story in the international climate change institutions is paralysis and fear of power, not bureaucracy run amok.

Experience in other areas of international environmental law strongly suggests that an independent international analytical body that adds value to raw reported data can lead to improved data quality as well as better international agreements. In the effort to regulate acid rain in Europe, for example, an international monitoring, modeling, and assessment program helped fill gaps in data and identify additional data that would be needed, and ultimately made it possible to set regulatory goals according to rational environmental criteria rather than simple and arbitrary emission targets. The institutionalized program transformed a skeletal regulatory system that was merely a postbox where countries sent their data into one that is, today, much more efficient and capable in aiding European societies to identify and achieve demanding international environmental goals. One result from that process is the 1994 "second sulfur protocol," a sophisticated and relatively efficient agreement that will achieve ambitious environmental goals. In contrast, a decade earlier the 1985 "first sulfur protocol" imposed a blunt and largely ineffective across-the-board cut in emissions that was motivated by neither particular ecological goals nor much economic analysis.[5]

As the stakes rise, the need for useful shared data sets and analytical tools will grow. Knowing this, a more intensive effort to build better data sets must begin now. The political showstopper of the Russia and Ukraine windfalls is but one illustration of why negotiators will be unable to allocate burdens without adequate data and analytical capacity in place. Better and shared knowledge about the Russian and Ukrainian futures could have reduced this political catastrophe. More generally, better information on costs and potential future emissions can reduce the tendency for negotiations over a fixed resource—such as the allocation of permits—to yield deadlock. Especially when negotiations aim to distribute a semipermanent asset, each party will assume the worst-case scenario—as discussed earlier, uncertain emission projections and unknown costs will lead parties to overstate future emissions and demand permits. Data programs are unable to solve this problem, but they can reduce the tendency for negotiations to slide into negative-sum bargaining. Improved data and analytical capacity can also enable sophisticated multi-issue bargains that link climate policy to other issues, which could make it easier to identify and negotiate positive-sum deals.

Third, and most important, new thinking is needed about the architecture of the treaty that will be used to control emissions. The problems that confront international emission trading are extremely difficult to solve. Trying to solve them in time to bring the Kyoto Protocol into legal force—especially when the best solutions defy conventional wisdom and require renegotiating central elements of Kyoto's commitments—is a recipe for failure. Few of the lessons learned from national trading systems can be transferred directly to international trading because the institutional setting of international law is radically different from national law. In the international system, parties can opt out of inconvenient international legal commitments much more easily than in a well-functioning national legal and political system.

I have suggested that the best "new thinking" starts by scrapping the idea of inviolable emission quantity targets and replacing it with a system that sets targets for the price as well as the quantity of emissions. I have argued that none of the market-based alternatives—neither pure emission trading, nor pure emission taxes—is feasible to implement. The hybrid price and quantity approach makes it possible to combine the best of both. That hybrid can make use of some aspects of the Kyoto Protocol, such as the CDM and especially the data reporting system, but fundamentally it would require a substantial restructuring of the way that global warming commitments are negotiated and codified into international law. That change cannot originate with academics—it must be the result of a reasoned debate and, ultimately, implemented by governments. The collapse of the Kyoto Protocol offers a propitious opportunity to conduct that debate.

Pressure for new thinking must begin with the United States government, which largely created the conventional wisdom that pure textbook emission trading is the best approach and has been the single most influential country in the negotiations to create global warming agreements. The United States has rightly held firm in requiring the use of market-based mechanisms to ensure that abatement of greenhouse gases is cost effective. Wrongly, it has advocated trading as the only market-based approach.

Coherent and realistic thinking from the European Union is also badly needed. European pressure was the main reason for the strict emission targets adopted in Kyoto. Yet the EU had no idea how it would achieve the target it proposed (a 15% cut in emissions). The strict target has accelerated interest in trading; yet until recently the EU has maintained that trading would be a loophole and should be barred (except for the pooling of permits among members of the EU, which the EU has embraced as part of the Union's common market). Today, the EU is reversing course as a growing number of EU members have realized that they cannot meet their targets without trading. But this awareness has triggered an odd response. The EU is now simultaneously embracing and hobbling the concept of trading. It has proposed to create an international emission trading system within the Kyoto Protocol but cap the level of trading. A cap on trading, EU policy makers hope, would limit the windfall of credits that Russia and Ukraine can sell to the West and force a minimum level of effort by Western nations within their own borders.[6] In reality, such caps are arbitrary and would cause more harm than good—they would ensure that the windfall permits given to Russia and Ukraine drive the more costly bona fide permits out of circulation. The EU is right to insist that textbook emission trad-

115

ing is not best for slowing global warming, but it has done little to advance serious thinking about the alternatives.

The story about Kyoto is not how hard the negotiators worked, but how easy it was. Progress was rapid, and the speedy creation of an emission trading system seemed too good to be true. It was.

The Causes and Effects of Global Warming: A Brief Survey of the Science

This book is about the design of an international architecture for managing the problem of global warming. In this appendix, very briefly, I give an overview of the state of scientific research on the global warming problem itself.

Since the industrial revolution, humans have burned ever greater quantities of fossil fuels (coal, oil, and natural gas) for energy. These fuels are principally made of carbon, which oxidizes to carbon dioxide (CO_2) when burnt. Coal is the most carbon-intensive fuel—compared with natural gas, coal yields about twice the emissions of CO_2 per unit of useful energy. Over three-quarters of today's net emissions of carbon dioxide are the consequence of burning fossil fuels, which is why dealing with the global warming problem is broadly synonymous with "decarbonizing" the world's energy system.[1]

The remaining one-quarter of net CO_2 emissions is a by-product of how humans alter the landscape. Vegetation, such as trees, contains large amounts of carbon, as do the surrounding soils. Burning or decay releases the carbon to the atmosphere. However, ecosystems also absorb carbon through photosynthesis as they grow, and it is the net effect that matters most.[2]

The processes that permanently remove these human emissions of CO_2 from the atmosphere operate slowly, which is why the atmospheric concentration of carbon dioxide has risen steadily over the last century. The process is akin to a bathtub with a slow drain—and a faucet that is opened ever wider as emissions increase.

By far, carbon dioxide is the most important cause of global warming. However, several other gases are minor actors in the drama. These include methane (CH_4) and nitrous oxide (N_2O). Even more minor are gases such as chlorofluorocarbons (CFCs), hydrochlorofluorocarbons (HCFCs), hydrofluorocarbons (HFCs), perfluorocarbons (PFCs), and sulfur hexafloride (SF_6).[3] CFCs and HCFCs also contribute to depletion of the ozone layer and are already tightly regulated under the Montreal Protocol on Substances that Deplete the Ozone Layer. That is why efforts to manage the global warming problem exclude CFCs and HCFCs and focus only on the other gases.

Every projection for future climate requires, first, a projection of future emissions and concentrations of carbon dioxide and other greenhouse gases. Analysts have developed various techniques for making such projections, but the task is tricky because the projections must extend out fifty years and beyond. Over such long time periods many factors, notably energy technologies, can change dramatically, and such changes have a huge impact on projected emissions.[4]

The temperature and climate of Earth are the by-product of the planet's energy balance. Incoming energy from the sun warms the planet, which radiates energy back to space. So long as incoming and outgoing radiation are in balance, the Earth's temperature stays constant. Most solar energy is visible, but the outward radiation occurs in the "infrared" part of the energy spectrum—like the infrared warmth from a hot water bottle, this outgoing radiation is invisible to human eyes. Greenhouse gases absorb some of this outgoing infrared radiation and prevent it from escaping directly to space, which alters Earth's energy balance and causes the planet to warm. The process has been dubbed the "greenhouse effect," although a greenhouse actually keeps its innards warm through a completely different mechanism. There is a large natural greenhouse effect that is essential to most life on Earth. Water vapor, CO_2, and other greenhouse gases occur naturally in the atmosphere and keep Earth's temperature about 34°C warmer than if the atmosphere contained no greenhouse gases. Without the greenhouse effect, Earth would be an icy and inhospitable ball in space. The global warming hypothesis maintains that human-caused emissions of greenhouse gases will intensify this natural greenhouse effect and make the planet less hospitable for humans and Nature. I will use the term "global warming" to describe this hypothesis, but a more accurate term would be "climate change" since changes in Earth's energy balance will affect many aspects of climate, not only temperature. Indeed, climatic changes may actually lead to lower local temperatures in some areas, even as the average temperature of the planet increases.

Over the last 120 years, as the concentration of greenhouse gases in the atmosphere has grown, the planet's temperature has also increased about 0.6°C. That may not sound like a lot, but small changes in average temperature correspond with large differences in climate. Only a few degrees of average temperature separate today's climate from that in the depth of the last glacial period about 20,000 years ago.

One challenge for the global warming hypothesis is that, historically, greenhouse gas concentrations and temperature have not moved in lockstep. For example, even though there has been a somewhat steady rise in the concentration of greenhouse gases, from 1900 to 1910 Earth's average temperature appears to have declined and, from 1940 to 1980, temperatures remained approximately level.[5] The global warming hypothesis acknowledges that many factors affect temperature—for example, changes in the Earth's orbit and variations in solar intensity—but that rising concentrations of greenhouse gases cause Earth's temperature to be higher than it would be otherwise. Computerized "general circulation models" (GCMs) are used to sort out these many influences on climate. Over the last decade, scientists working with GCMs have linked at least some of the observed rise in temperature to the accumulation of greenhouse gases in the atmosphere. Having spotted the "fingerprint" of humankind's emissions, scientists now have greater confidence that the computer models that are being used to explain current and past climatology of Earth can also be used to make useful projections for the future. Nonetheless, there are still many uncertainties and the projections are far from airtight.[6]

Even greater uncertainities arise in the next step: to demonstrate that changing climates create hazards for humans and Nature. Such research requires linking together many intellectual disciplines and models, which propagates and multiplies uncertainty in the results. The largest challenge in this research is to account for the fact that humans and Nature adapt to change. If we suddenly imposed drought on Iowa farmers then surely they would be affected. But if reduced rainfall and higher temperatures became more likely over a long period of time—and if farmers knew that these new conditions were soon to arrive—they could adapt by planting different seeds or shifting from farming altogether. Nature also adapts to change, although it does not have the capacity to look ahead and anticipate the direction of change.[7]

In general, wealthy countries have greater capacity for adaptation. In addition, the fraction of economic activity that depends upon climate and is therefore especially vulnerable to changing weather is much smaller in industrialized countries than in the developing world. In many developing countries over half the economic output is agricultural and potentially vulnerable to the weather; in advanced industrialized nations that fraction is typically about 2%. These factors—higher exposure and lower capacity to adapt—explain why most studies conclude that developing countries are more vulnerable to the effects of global warming. However, even that conclusion is contested. Advanced industrialized countries have large amounts of valuable capital stock (buildings, highways, etc.) near coastlines—vulnerable to rising sea levels and coastal storms. (Evidence that sea levels rise when temperatures increase is extremely good, although large uncertainties remain; evidence that storminess will increase is still shaky.) Thus the absolute value of the impacts of global warming may be larger in the advanced industrialized countries while the fraction of total economic activity affected is larger in the developing world.[8]

Much of the analysis of the effects of climate change has focused on gradual and somewhat predictable effects such as changes in temperature, rainfall patterns, and rising sea levels. However, various severe and nonlinear effects may also occur. For example, higher temperatures may severely slow the circulation of the North Atlantic Ocean, and there is evidence that such a shutdown has occurred due to natural changes in climate in the past.[9] Other "catastrophic" changes may occur to ecosystems if they are pushed beyond their capacity to adapt.[10] Such changes, because they typically entail many nonlinear interactions, are difficult to quantify. Each, individually, may have a low probability of occurrence, but if the building concentrations of greenhouse gases trigger them then the consequences could be very severe and perhaps irreversible. Economic analysis suggests that such "low probability, high consequence" risks greatly increase the level of effort that countries should make to control emissions of greenhouse gases.[11]

Afterword

The hardcover edition of this book appeared early in 2001, on the heels of two events that would prove important for the fate of the Kyoto Protocol. One was the sixth session of the Conference of the Parties held in The Hague. COP-6, as it was known, had been billed as the capstone to a long diplomatic process of filling in the details of the Kyoto Protocol. Back in 1997 when diplomats had inked the protocol, they had gone right to the wire—actually a few hours past—just in their efforts to frame the broad contours of the Kyoto deal. They agreed on emission targets for 38 industrialized countries; they embraced, in principle, the idea of international trading of emission credits; they accepted that developing countries would not be asked to limit their emissions. On pretty much everything else of consequence, the Kyoto negotiations ran out of time. As usually happens in tricky bargaining situations, matters on which no agreement could be crafted in Kyoto were reclassified as "details" and pushed into the future.

Among the many details that were left unsettled were rules for emission trading, mechanisms for enforcing compliance, and procedures for crediting the reduction of emissions from projects in developing countries—all essential to understanding the real cost of implementing Kyoto as well as its real impact on the problem of global warming. Rather than limping over the finish line at Kyoto in the wee hours of the morning on December 11, 1997, diplomats had sounded the starting gun for a longer process, with less firm deadlines, to transform these broad contours of an agreement into something that serious governments could actually ratify and implement. COP-6, three years later in 2000, emerged as the deadline for those events. "Work it out!" was the official slogan of The Hague meeting—printed on the cover of every notepad and blazed across banners in the main hall.

Unfolding at the same time as COP-6 was the U.S. presidential election. Normally, Americans vote for their president the first Tuesday after the first Monday in November, and they know the result that evening. But confusing ballots and antiquated counting machines, notably in Palm Beach County, Florida, delivered no firm verdict for the contenders, George W. Bush and Al Gore. Only a month later, on December 12, did the U.S. Supreme Court finally settle the matter for Bush. In the midst of all this, diplomats arrived in The Hague with the goal of limping over yet another finish line.

Voting mishaps in Florida created a severe problem for the U.S. delegation, as they were negotiating on behalf of an unknown boss. If Gore took the prize, then U.S. climate policy would continue largely uninterrupted. Gore was already vice president and controlled the climate issue within the White House; the U.S. diplomats who arrived in The Hague were, in effect, already working for Al Gore. They plausibly argued that a successful deal would free the new president to submit Kyoto and the legislation that would be needed to put Kyoto into practice to the U.S. Congress for approval. At the time of COP-6, only small developing countries (plus Mexico) had actually ratified Kyoto—for them the decision was relatively easy because compliance with Kyoto required little effort. For the industrialized countries, however, adhering to Kyoto's commitments could be quite demanding, and all held back ratification until agreement on the fine print. In this process, the United States was not visibly a laggard, although the U.S. Senate had signaled back in the summer of 1997 (before Kyoto) with a 95–0 resolution that it would refuse any treaty that did not put meaningful limits on emissions from developing countries. Kyoto didn't do that and seemed to fail the test, but nobody was sure at the time exactly what even a president supportive of the goals of Kyoto could usher through the Congress.

The protocol would have required the United States to reduce its emissions of carbon dioxide and the other gases that cause global warming to about 7% below 1990 levels by the year 2010. By the eve of COP-6 at The Hague, U.S. emissions had already risen 13% above 1990s levels and were on track to rise another 12% during the next decade. The good news was that the rate at which emissions were rising was less than one-third the bullish growth rate of the U.S. economy—indeed, ever since the energy shocks of the early 1970s had created an urgent incentive to conserve, nearly all industrialized nations had partially decoupled growth in their economies from the growth in consumption of energy and the emissions that are a by-product of burning fossil fuels. But the bad news was that America's emission trajectory was still pointing upward, despite the Kyoto Protocol's aim of making it slope down. And the Kyoto commitments would come due in less than a decade—too rapid for much response in the energy system. Four-fifths of the power plants that were expected to be in operation in 2010 were already in operation or under construction. Following any realistic political timetable, the mechanisms needed to implement Kyoto within the United States would not be credibly in place until 2003 or 2004 at the earliest; by then, most of the automobiles that would be

125

on the road in 2008 when the Kyoto targets took effect would have rolled off the assembly lines. Other countries were in similar (if less dire) circumstances.

Unable to have much effect on the near-term trajectory of emissions, America's diplomats in The Hague were nonetheless faced with the task of crafting a deal that would allow the United States to ratify and implement its Kyoto commitments. Their best hope was to get agreement on full and free use of emission trading, which would make it possible for Americans to purchase credits (mainly from Russia and Ukraine) to cover their deficit. The American diplomats also sought liberal crediting for the carbon that is stored in forests, cropland, and grazing pastures. In the United States and every other industrialized country, forests were already growing larger and denser, and farmers were already adopting better land-management practices. Clever accounting and lenient rules could allow countries to claim huge credits for these activities and encourage additional efforts at sequestering carbon, which would make it much easier to meet the Kyoto targets. In the wee hours of the morning on the final day of COP-6, the United States and key members of the European Union had reached a deal, only to see that arrangement fall apart a few hours later when the European Union backed away. It was a strange and dark moment. Strange because the United States probably never could have implemented the deal it had offered. Even with substantial carbon credits and huge purchases of credits from Russia and Ukraine, U.S. lawmakers were unlikely to approve an arrangement that seemed to involve accounting tricks and sending billions of dollars overseas just to assure compliance on paper. Dark because the deal—which offered probably more than the best that the European Union could have hoped for from the United States—fell apart when key EU members were unable to sort out their own affairs and negotiate as a unit. In the months after COP-6, the real problems with the EU position grew even darker, as it became clear that unrealistic Green Party positions, prosecuted notably by France, were at the root of the EU split.

In March 2001 the new Bush administration withdrew from Kyoto. A firestorm of criticism followed—some of it properly focused on the administration's apparent disdain for international cooperation and much of it animated by the belief that Kyoto was viable if not for George W. Bush. A week after the U.S. exit, I wrote an article for the *New York Times* that echoed the premise of this book.[1] My argument, foreshadowed in chapter 1, was that U.S. compliance with the Kyoto commitments was feasible only through accounting tricks and by moving piles of money to Russia and Ukraine in exchange for bogus emission credits. Why, I asked, would we want to embrace a fraudulent framework for our first step on a century-long journey of decarbonizing the energy system? The real test for serious climate policy was not adherence to Kyoto. Overly ambitious and wrongheaded efforts at treaty building often fail, and the sooner we look beyond to new structures, the sooner we can construct something that would be effective. The real test, I argued, was the Bush administration's next move. Unhappy with what they saw in Kyoto, what was their vision for the path beyond? The administration, it seemed, liked the piece and sent copies worldwide to their diplomatic missions.

The EU was in a different position through all this. The European public cared a lot more about the problem of climate change, in part because Europe may actually be more vulnerable to the effects of rising sea levels, storms, and perhaps even drought. Real or not, press coverage of the issue often linked extreme weather events—such as floods in 1998 and the heat wave during the summer of 2003—to climate change. In contrast, ever since the hot summer of 1988, the U.S. press has never given sustained attention to the impacts of climate change. Having lived on both sides of the Atlantic during this period, it is striking how the European newspapers report the new findings

127

of climate science almost weekly, especially in Britain (which has become Europe's true leader on this issue—leading by example with aggressive and often thoughtful policies). American news, by contrast, is relatively silent.

The European political system is also organized quite differently from America's, and that provides more space for organized environmental opinion. The parliamentary system has allowed green parties to gain power through coalition governments, and inevitably they have a large say over environmental policy; fighting global warming, for many of these parties, is a central guiding principle—it informs everything from energy policy to diplomatic strategy. Mandates for renewable energy and energy efficiency all find their root in climate change. And Kyoto had become the keystone for climate policy in Europe; no matter what the United States said, Kyoto, to the Europeans, was sacred. The rising power of Brussels also played a role, since implementation of Kyoto would require the European Union to act as a single unit; a competent, professional bureaucracy in Brussels kept that effort on track and ensured, for example, that even as the EU presidency rotated every six months, the EU's representatives kept the same tune. During stressful moments when time was tight, the many colors of the EU exploded—as at The Hague—but Kyoto was a unifying theme and Brussels, the unifier.

Outside Brussels, George W. Bush was probably the single strongest force for unity behind Kyoto. His blunt exit from the regime redoubled efforts within the EU and other key industrialized nations—notably Canada and Japan—to find a way beyond the impasse at The Hague. They reconvened in Bonn during the summer of 2001, at a meeting inelegantly titled "COP-6*bis*," and quickly found agreement on a deal that was nearly identical to what had been declared unacceptable in The Hague just six months earlier. As in the failed deal at The Hague, special credits for carbon in forests and soils were awarded most liberally to the countries that were most reluctant to join the party—Canada and Japan assured special allocations for themselves. In a truly bizarre twist of fate that revealed that governments often do not prosecute their own best strategies, Russia also demanded (and got) a large allocation for forest carbon. Russia's forests were, indeed, growing; but Russia's real problem at the time was that the U.S. exit had already left it with a vast over-supply of emission credits that seemed likely to crash prices; the last thing Russia needed was still more credits. The final deal on the enforcement mechanism required any country that overshot its Kyoto obligations to repay its violation with a 30% penalty in the future. This arrangement of shifting penalties into the future would exacerbate what I call "negative-sum" allocation (see chapter 2). Any government that fears overshooting its allocation of emission quotas from the first period (2008–2012) would simply demand a more generous quota for the future. Since the amount of overshoot is intrinsically uncertain—it depends on the vagaries of the economy and technology—the cautious government will imagine the worst-case scenario and then add the penalty (30%) to that result. Kyoto's architects thought they were clever in demanding that future allocations be set in a process that was to begin no later than 2005—long before Kyoto's first budget period. But that was an empty and wrongheaded mandate. Empty because deadlines are often broken in international diplomacy. Wrongheaded because the earlier the deadline, the greater the uncertainty, which would actually magnify the problem of negative-sum bargaining.[2] Using this book as a basis, I made these arguments in the spring of 2001, in the aftermath of the Bush bailout and the run-up to COP-6*bis*. In the shrill environment of the time, where words against Kyoto were heresy, I had no impact.

The single worst day for Kyoto was September 11, 2001. As the Twin Towers fell, Americans understandably focused on new priorities. The final meeting in Bush's cabinet-level process for developing a new climate policy had been scheduled for that week. Who knows what they would have decided, but it is certain that without the eclipse of September 11 the Bush administration would have been under pressure to provide something credible. Until that defining moment, the U.S. government was severely isolated on this issue; domestic opposition to the Bush policy was well organized. But when Americans instantly refocused their attention—first to terror, then to war, and then also to the ailing economy—the broad public pressure that had been mounting for credible policy on climate change evaporated quickly. Only people who didn't vote for Bush—and who were still burning with anger over an election they viewed as stolen—were hot for action on global warming. Nobody else cared, and those who did care were irrelevant for the mavens at the top of the political party that controlled the White House and Congress. The predictable result, unveiled finally in February 2002, was a series of voluntary measures and underfunded technology programs designed mainly to give the appearance of a credible response. The president boldly announced his intention to cut the "carbon intensity" of the U.S. economy—that is, emissions normalized per unit of economic output—by 18% over the next decade. I wrote an op-ed piece for the *Washington Post* attacking the policy as unserious and pointing out that ever since 1922 the U.S. economy has, on average, cut carbon intensity by about 18% every decade.[3] The administration didn't send that op-ed around to its diplomatic outposts.

Among the many effects of September 11 was its convenient political cover for American hostility to international institutions. Any fair reading of history would see that hostility as part of a durable pattern in which powerful states pursue their interests, aligning with international institutions only when it is convenient to do so. Thus the United States and the EU together pursued their war in Kosovo largely without the "legitimacy" of the UN; they sought instead a more convenient legitimacy in NATO. But the American wars and isolation following September 11 brought into stark relief the fact that the United States and Europe were following different trajectories in their ability to exert influence over world events—as evident in the stunningly rapid military victories in Afghanistan and Iraq. (The postwar periods are not unfolding so neatly, but such events are still taking shape.) America the powerful can do what it wants, even when it acts largely alone; the EU, by contrast, has embraced a different philosophy in which international law rather than economic and military prowess keep order in the international system. Robert Kagan has written a convincing book on this subject.[4]

Kyoto is a strong test for the thesis of different trajectories. There are few other areas of budding international law and procedure where the United States is more isolated. Even the United Kingdom, the solid "other pole" in the U.S.-led "coalition of the willing" that overran Saddam Hussein, is an ardent defender of Kyoto. Yet the only thing that Kyoto's supporters can say that is positive about America's role in Kyoto is that the U.S. government is not actively interfering with the effort to build an international regime to combat climate change. I'm not sure that even that faint praise is awarded correctly. At the COP-8 meeting in Delhi, India (in fall 2002), the United States and India helped to organize a coalition that reaffirmed the developing countries' wariness of undertaking the Kyoto commitments. Such ventures worry me, as it is not in the U.S. interest to animate an already overly focused coalition of developing countries in favor of inaction.

America's engagement with the world will sort itself out over time as the campaign of antiterror and hostility toward international institutions stretches beyond reason; the backlash, already evident, will reset priorities. But the estrangement of Kyoto is likely to be more durable, and the need for both sides of the Atlantic to understand each other's predicament and constraints has become more urgent.

As a guest of the U.S. State Department I traveled to several European capitals and to Brussels a few weeks after September 11. My goal was simply to talk with senior European officials about their strategy for the road ahead and their views of the

131

United States. The COP-6*bis* meeting in Bonn had ended just before the traditional holiday month of August, so European capitals had really just begun at that moment to contemplate the implications of their success in finalizing the Kyoto details—albeit, success minus the United States. Everywhere I went, the prevailing hypothesis was that the shock of September 11 would make the United States realize the need for a broad program of international cooperation; reconstruction of Kyoto and numerous other international projects would all follow. European hopes for reform were projected onto the shock of September 11. I argued that the events were unrelated—September 11 would not save Kyoto. Indeed, we have since seen that September 11 merely accelerated the divergence of trajectories. The EU needed the United States as a credible member of Kyoto. Bashing America had been a convenient way to rally Kyoto's supporters, but rallying the troops for an empty war was no way to get started on solving the climate problem, and anyone serious about solving the climate problem knew that America needed to figure prominently in the solution.

Of course it is wrong to discuss "Europeans" as a monolith—just as "Americans" are not of one view—but I find that it is still hard for many Europeans to understand the shock and immediate reorientation of American priorities after September 11. Flying back to the United States from that sojourn on Air France, I asked the pilots if they would mind my sitting up front to watch the landing.[5] (U.S. airlines had long banned that practice, but the European carriers generally had more flexible rules.) To my astonishment they said yes. We flew the famous "Canarsie" approach into Kennedy Airport, which involves flying west over the water and then making a sweeping right turn before landing to the northeast. Yet here I was looking out the left window of the cockpit as we turned in for landing—staring at the empty, still-smoldering space in downtown Manhattan where the Twin Towers had been felled by guys who had forced their way into airliner cockpits—wondering why these pilots let me join them in the front. By instinct, no American pilot or airline would have allowed any stranger in the cockpit. (Air France has since changed its procedures.)

Beyond Kyoto

Other than the grubby desire to boost sales, why reissue a book that was written before this important string of events—COP-6 at The Hague, the Bush administration's exit, the reinvigoration of Kyoto in Bonn, and September 11? The answer is that the central argument I make in these pages is as relevant today as it was in November 2000, when Princeton University Press finalized the page proofs. The need for clear thinking on why the architecture of Kyoto is failing is essential to framing more effective alternatives for the future.

No matter what happens with the Kyoto Protocol itself, action and diplomacy on climate change are already oriented beyond Kyoto. Even as most industrialized nations have remained formally within the Kyoto system, their actual efforts to control emissions are mainly calibrated by their own assessments of the best effort that their populations are willing to support, rather than the specific obligations under Kyoto. Japan's response has been to develop an ambitious plan that is formally focused on compliance with Kyoto. On paper, Japan's plan is perhaps the most costly of any advanced industrialized nation, probably because Japan hosted the Kyoto conference; in practice, the actual Japanese effort is already shrinking, as grand visions for changing behavior and for making extensive use of new nuclear power supplies are not realized. In Japan, the government must pretend to take the Kyoto targets seriously even as real action falls short. The most interesting of these "best efforts" approaches is in the European Union, which has delivered a comprehensive program that involves voluntary and mandatory regulations to control emissions from transportation, buildings, and small industrial sources, with the rest controlled through an innovative emission trading system (ETS). The year 2005 will mark the start of a trial phase in the EU's ETS. Several European countries, notably the UK, have already started their own trading systems. At this writing (March 2004) members of the EU are still preparing their national plans for allocating emission permits and managing the trading system within their borders. Not surprisingly, these plans are slipping behind the strict schedule mandated by Brussels, and have become lightning rods for controversy. The ETS requires the European member states to allocate emission permits worth potentially hundreds of billions of dollars and to assure the integrity of this new system for trading property rights. The difficulty even in Europe—where most governments are competent, the European legal context is sound, and Brussels provides a backstop—should be a warning to any government that attempts to create an effective emission trading system without assuring that a sound institutional context is first in place.

Having conducted dozens of interviews in Japan and the EU, my sense is that these governments are probably implementing policies that are comparable to what they would have implemented without Kyoto's entering into force. These countries are responding to public pressure that is reflected in a wide array of declarations and policy platforms, including the Kyoto Protocol itself. In some cases, Kyoto has played a modest role as a catalyst or channel for political influence. But we must not forget that, at the same time that Kyoto was taking shape, many governments—notably in Europe—were already preparing policies that they would implement regardless of whether any treaty had emerged from the diplomatic process.

The only area where the world has not yet moved "beyond Kyoto" is in the formal legal status of the Kyoto commitments. When the United States crudely left the Kyoto framework, it became politically impossible for others to contemplate any alternative course but to rally support for the Kyoto Protocol. At the same time, it became much easier for these governments to pursue autarkic policies while nonetheless assuring their compliance with their Kyoto commitments. The key to this new political logic is the option for trading emission credits. Russia and Ukraine envisioned that they would hold a surplus that could approach 1 billion metric tons of carbon (3.7 billion tons of CO_2). Before the United States unambiguously left the Kyoto framework, its demand for permits was expected to be about the same magnitude, and most observers thought that prices would rise. Without the United States, however, total demand from the remaining buyers—in Canada, the European Union, and Japan—is unlikely to exceed 200 million tons of carbon (730 million tons of CO_2) and will probably be much lower.

Although this new situation made it easier for Canada, Europe, and Japan to assure compliance, it also created a severe crisis for any nation that sought to implement Kyoto at face value. Allowing truly open international trade would produce a flood of emission permits that could make it much cheaper for firms to purchase credits from Russia and Ukraine than to spend resources on anything except truly costless emission control at home. This was terrible news for Russia, which saw the value of its potential windfall tumble from tens of billions of dollars to something on the order of 100 million dollars or probably much less. For the other countries that stayed inside Kyoto, the outcome was equally catastrophic because the vast over-supply of Russian and Ukrainian permits could undermine the carefully built constituency for meaningful action on climate change. Those same countries not only saw their efforts for 2008–2012 undermined, but any Russian and Ukrainian permits not spent during that first budget period would be banked for the future—undermining potential future action as well.

Every country that has faced this problem has adopted the easiest and most effective response: they have not embraced international emission trading. Japan's vision for compliance involves no use of trading. The EU envisions no trading for two-thirds of EU emissions. For the remaining one-third, the

AFTERWORD

European emission trading system is ringed with a carefully constructed wall that will trigger special reviews if the quantity of permits traded exceeds 6% of the permits in circulation. Fearful of the flood, these countries have sought to regulate their exposure carefully.

This response illustrates the central argument of this book, which is as relevant today as it was when Kyoto was taking shape. Governments care about cost. Those that are most savvy about their commitments will tune the mechanisms of implementation so that they impose costs that are comparable with the public's willingness to pay. First and foremost, governments make these decisions themselves and do not delegate that authority to international institutions. In the aftermath of Kyoto, the willing governments that have stayed inside the Kyoto framework have tweaked the rules so that costs actually *rise*— so that the government is seen to undertake meaningful action. The scenario that preoccupied me in this book was different— if the United States stayed in, how could governments be certain that costs would not spiral out of control? How could governments assure that costs would not rise above their willingness to pay, forcing governments either to abrogate or exit their international commitments?

My response to these central questions was to embrace a hybrid approach to emission trading. In this system, governments would coordinate not only in setting limits on total emissions (as in Kyoto); they would also commit to issue new permits at an agreed price. That is, if the cost of compliance proved to be low, then the system would behave like a textbook system of emission trading where each nation would stay at or below its cap—much as we see in the Kyoto system today without any U.S. demand for emission credits. If costs rose higher than governments were willing to pay, then the system would behave like a tax, as each new ton of emissions would incur a known cost. In chapter 4 I explain this system in more detail. Others have also done admirable work on this concept, often calling it a "safety valve."[6]

Critics have charged that this system is weak and complicated. As for the first charge, I am guilty only in a public international lawyer's dream world. It is true that a system that imposed "top down" a set of binding limits on emissions according to strict targets and timetables could yield tighter control on emissions. But such a system is impossible to install within the international system as it is currently organized. Nations, especially powerful nations, can easily avoid international commitments that are inconvenient. Look no further than the U.S. exit from Kyoto as proof. The system that was left after the U.S. exit was laden with such a large surplus of emission credits that if the remaining nations had actually implemented the treaty literally, the effect on emissions would be much less than the actual policy programs that key industrialized countries are now implementing. It is fashionable to criticize the United States as a cowboy-rejecter of international norms, but similar behavior is seen in the failure of France and Germany to keep their public deficits in line with the strictures of the European Monetary Union. In both situations, inconvenient international commitments have spurred nations to exit (as in the United States) or to attempt to escape inconvenient penalties for noncompliance (as in France and Germany). Eventually France and Germany may be forced to pay because enforcers within the European Monetary Union have recourse to the European Court of Justice. No comparable institution exists in the Kyoto framework.

I was drawn to the hybrid system because, unlike a simple cap on emissions, a hybrid approach would make it much easier to tailor international commitments to national willingness to pay. International institutions are most effective when they help nations craft and implement commitments that are closest to the frontier of what each is willing to do for the collective effort. Greater certainty about the marginal cost of emissions would translate into greater certainty about the total cost of controlling emissions, which in turn would ease the task of selecting international commitments that match the national willingness

137

to pay. (A simple carbon tax could have the same effect. However, as I show in chapter 3, it is not feasible to monitor and enforce compliance with an internationally coordinated carbon tax system.)

The hybrid is not a panacea. The construction of any effective trading system—hybrid or not—will require starting with countries that share a comparable willingness to pay. The inclusion of nations that are averse to costly commitments—like Russia and Ukraine in Kyoto, or developing countries in the future— leads to what I call in this book a "negative-sum" negotiating dynamic. Each new entrant demands as many emission credits as its worst-case expectations for future emissions. Since these nations have a wide band of possible future emissions, each will demand an unreasonably high allocation. Economists have tended to focus only on gains from trade and thus have advocated the widest possible emission trading system. But the other side of the equation is interest and capacity to make the trading system effective. Countries without interest in controlling emissions will undermine a wide trading system by demanding large allocations, which will assure that the trading system has no effect on global emissions. Countries without the capacity to enforce the integrity of the trading system will need to rely heavily on international institutions, which rarely have the capacity to inspect and enforce. Often, interest and capacity are correlated. The existence of weak public institutions often explains why a country's economy is relatively small, and a low level of economic activity often explains why the public places a low value on protection of global environmental amenities. As the Kyoto negotiations were taking shape, a debate emerged between "broad then deep" and "deep then broad" approaches to building effective international regimes. The logic I present here argues strongly for the latter—apply substantive commitments, first, to like-minded countries that share a positive willingness to pay. Creating an effective system will be hard enough without inviting foxes into the henhouse.

As for the charge that the hybrid system is complicated, my response is that it is essential to compare the task at hand with the appropriate precedents. When most environmentalists and environmental diplomats approached the problem of global warming, the precedent they had in mind was the Montreal Protocol on Substances that Deplete the Ozone Layer (1987). I explain in chapter 1 why the lessons learned from that model are inapplicable to the case of global warming. Not only is the economic context for controlling CO_2 completely different from that for controlling ozone-depleting substances, but the conventional wisdom derived from the Montreal experience is based on a misreading of history. The Montreal Protocol has been effective not simply by setting aggressive goals that forced firms to innovate and apply new technologies; it also made it possible for governments to accept aggressive goals because the treaty includes a special exemption for "essential uses" in cases where new technologies did not arrive on the marketplace at acceptable cost. In other terms, the "essential-use" mechanism has served the very same purpose as the hybrid safety-valve system advocated in this book. If costs rose to a level higher than what the key countries were willing to pay, then the "essential-use" exemption would prevent the Montreal treaty system from provoking a backlash by forcing governments nonetheless to phase out particular uses of these substances that would be technically difficult to replace.

The most appropriate lessons will be found not in international environmental cooperation but in the areas of international trade and monetary policy. In those areas, governments have adopted commitments that affect the core of their economies, just as regulation of CO_2 will affect how modern economies metabolize energy from fossil fuels. Progress was slow. The WTO, for example, is the result of five decades of institution building that began with a small group of like-minded countries convened originally under the General Agreement on Tariffs and Trade (GATT). (GATT itself was a by-product of a much bolder vision for an International Trade Organization; like Kyoto, the ITO vision proved to be too ambitious and politically unrealistic at the time.)

Creating a cost-sensitive emission trading system is probably most similar to the creation of a new international currency. Governments that are serious about assuring the integrity of this new currency won't invite a large number of nations with different (often competing) core interests and institutional capacities into the club. Rather, they will start with a zone of countries they can trust, since allowing exchange of a new currency creates not only opportunities for trade but also vulnerabilities if other countries undermine the scrip's value. Other currencies from outside this zone will be barred, traded under tight regulation, or exchanged at a discount. The European emission trading system is evolving exactly according to this paradigm; it is the single most important policy experiment to watch today. If the European system works, it can set the standard for other nations. In fact, the European currency could become the equivalent of a reserve currency for carbon—the standard-bearer for other currencies. Even if Kyoto fails to enter into force, the EU is likely to go ahead with its trading system. That scenario is probably the best case for the emergence of a truly effective trading system, since it would concentrate the most leverage over the system's design into the hands of an institution—the EU—that cares most about its success. In contrast, if Kyoto enters into force, the EU will be required to contend with a dysfunctional Clean Development Mechanism (CDM) and the possibly large volumes of emission credits from Russia that would probably be part of any deal needed to get Russia's ratification of Kyoto.

It is shameful that the United States is nowhere to be seen in this important creation of a new monetary system. America has a strong interest in creating its own currency—its own trading system, with a safety valve to protect against high costs.[7]

This bottom-up approach to emission trading creates little space for developing countries, at least in the initial stages. What should be done about them? The answer that I offer in this book may be misguided, although it is perhaps the only aspect of this book that has not attracted vehement criticism from the pro-Kyoto camp. My argument was that the solution that has been proffered by many American academics and government officials—to impose a cap on developing country emissions—would not be effective. The negative-sum dynamic would lead to excessive printing of this new currency, turning the whole scheme into a game for rent-seekers rather than a serious response to the threat of climate change. That conclusion still holds today. Instead, I argued that we must redouble efforts to make Kyoto's Clean Development Mechanism (CDM) work. I didn't see any alternative, as developing countries were already counting on the CDM to unlock large investment flows; indeed, at the time I wrote this book, many CDM projects were already under way. The idea behind the CDM seemed like a reasonable compromise. Instead of attempting the impossible task of imposing meaningful caps on total emissions from developing countries, the CDM would calculate the "baseline" of emissions in a developing country and then reward investors for particular individual projects that reduced emissions below the baseline.

The problem with the CDM is that it seems to have failed despite best efforts by the international community. Within the CDM itself, the political body that is charged with reviewing projects has approved only three projects out of two dozen that have been submitted—on grounds that the criteria for measuring the "baseline" of emissions is tricky to calculate robustly. Indeed, they are right to scrutinize baselines. In a modern economy that is open to international trade in investment and technology, how could anyone estimate the future level of emissions in the hypothetical contexts of "before" and "after" a discrete project? Indeed, the World Bank's Prototype Carbon Fund (PCF)—which has pooled money from a few key governments and firms to help jump start the CDM—has put the best accountants on the task and arrived at conflicting answers while revealing that rigorous baseline calculations will be very costly to make.[8]

In fact, the projects that are most likely to have the largest effect on developing country emissions are those for which it is most difficult to make baseline calculations. Those projects, in effect, permanently alter the baseline and lock in lower emission trajectories. They include, for example, early efforts in China to build a gas infrastructure. China's west-east gas pipeline along with the Chinese government's early rules to spur investment in terminals for liquefied natural gas (LNG) imports in southern coastal provinces are probably not economic by themselves, but they will create a commercial context for gas that will make future investments easier. Although China isn't pursuing CDM credit for these projects, in the CDM context China might claim that these early projects should merit CDM credit because they are not economic on their own. Yet it is impossible to estimate the true lock-in potential, as the strongest effects on Chinese CO_2 emissions will occur much later in projects that *are* economically viable on their own, thanks to these early loss-making infrastructure investments.

My colleagues at Stanford Law School (Professor Tom Heller) and the Indian Institute of Management in Ahmedabad (Professor P. R. Shukla) have suggested that governments adopt a "development-first" strategy with developing countries.[9] Heller and Shukla argue that, rather than attempting to create incentives for discrete new projects focused on particular quantified reductions in greenhouse gases, industrialized and developing countries should instead assemble broad packages of policies that are framed, at the outset, as development initiatives. Within broad development goals they should identify the many opportunities for low-carbon pathways—as evident in the earlier example of gas in China. Whereas the CDM's rules only allow credit for projects that are not economic on their own, this alternative "development-first" approach would focus on points where

142

carbon-saving and economy-growing opportunities are mutually reinforcing. The advantages of this approach are economic and bureaucratic. Economically, the CDM has not become such a powerful instrument that it affects development strategies; a concerted effort to build carbon reduction into mainstream development programs could have much more leverage over real investment patterns. Moreover, within developing countries, ministries charged with development are relatively powerful and can create coherent plans that lead to action, while the environmental ministries that often lead CDM projects have little clout. There is still much to be done to elaborate this idea; redoubling efforts in that direction might yield another fizzle as in the CDM. Of course, this approach will face some political difficulties since, by design, it will not yield specific and quantified emission reductions. I see that political barrier as one of salesmanship rather than policy architecture; any program that reflects the developing countries' desire to avoid costly commitments while also attempting to have a large impact on infrastructure investments will necessarily yield uncertain real impacts on emissions. That fact underscores the need to treat the problem of developing countries—or any reluctant participant in emission controls, such as Russia—with instruments that are separate from the quantified money-creating mechanisms of the hybrid system of emission trading that I advocate for the core.

In the highly politicized environment of the U.S. exit from Kyoto, this book attracted the most hostile responses from those who professed to be most concerned with the threats of global warming. That community had largely equated the mission of slowing global warming with the need to bring Kyoto into force. I have argued that no such equation exists. Today it is best to focus—slowly, but with conviction—on building a system that works for a limited number of like-minded countries. Hurried efforts to assemble complex coalitions with large numbers of countries and create expectations around slapdash systems will not work in practice and will probably delay the emergence of a

143

serious response to the threats of climate change. In making these arguments, I have eschewed diplomatic language; instead, I have focused on fundamentals and drawn bold and sharp lines. Actually putting these ideas into practice, of course, will require a different approach. Diplomats will need to transform them into less threatening concepts; they will need to show that they are mere tweaks to the mainstream. Such is the craft of diplomacy, and excellence at that craft is not the subject of this thin, directly argued book.

The first step beyond Kyoto is the realization that those governments that are actually implementing global warming policies are already operating far outside the Kyoto framework. In Europe, Canada, and Japan, these governments probably would have done something similar if the Kyoto Protocol had crashed back at Kyoto. Although the diplomats will probably call the successor agreement "Kyoto," the architects should start with the realization that the slate is remarkably clean. What comes next depends on a coherent plan of action and learning the right lessons from history. This book is a down payment in that direction.

Notes

1. There are some very important exceptions to this general statement that help to prove the rule. Some firms have moved ahead to control emissions because they view it as (a) a hedge against a future that might require rapid controls on emissions, (b) a way to spur their firms to use costly resources, such as fossil fuels, more efficiently, (c) good publicity, (d) a way to push policy makers to adopt certain types of emission controls—in particular, emission trading systems that allow these firms to gain credit for their "early action" to reduce emissions, and (e) the "right" thing to do. Other observers may have a slightly different list of reasons or a different emphasis, but it is undeniable that some firms are acting. Many have formed alliances that allow them to trade information and attract further publicity. Notably, see the Pew Center on Climate Change (www.pewclimate.org) and the recently announced partnership between Environmental Defense and several firms, many of which also participate in the Pew program (www.edf.org). The ED partnership includes specific targets for reducing emissions and the requirement that members publicly report their emissions.

2. These emission trends, their causes, and the prospects for complying with the Kyoto limits are described in much more detail in chapter 1. It is difficult to make definitive statements about what constitutes compliance, in part because countries may be able to take credit for carbon dioxide absorbed in forests and agricultural soils (so-called "carbon sinks"), but accounting rules for those credits have not been determined. In addition to complying through efforts entirely within their own borders, countries may also be able to take advantage of various forms of emission trading that would allow them to purchase credits overseas, but the rules for such trading also have not been established. Chapter 1 discusses these options in more detail.

3. There is no widely accepted definition of "industrialized" and "developing." My statement about emission trends is based on comparing emissions from the industrialized countries listed in "Annex I" of the Framework Convention on Climate Change with emissions from all the other nations. Annex I includes the advanced industrialized nations (Australia, Canada, Japan, New Zealand, United States, Western Europe) as well as the former centrally planned nations (Belarus, Eastern Europe, Russia, and Ukraine). The three-decade estimate is based on the projections of IIASA (the International Institute for Applied Systems Analysis) and the World Energy Council (Nakićenović et al., 1998). Other projections generally deliver similar results.

4. On fluxes, see Schimel et al. (1996) and numerous studies on particular gases and fluxes that I cite in chapter 3 of this book, including notably the work of Nilsson et al. (2000) on forests.

5. Schelling (1960); Olson (1965); Olson and Zeckhauser (1966); Raiffa (1982); Shubik (1982); Sebenius (1983); Oye (1986). A key problem for creating the rules for the CDM is how transaction costs affect the allocation of potential CDM credits. On transaction costs and bargaining, see especially Dixit (1996).

6. Weitzman (1974); Roberts and Spence (1976); Pigou ([1920/ 1932] 1952); Dales (1968); Coase (1960).

7. In economics, much of the focus has been on institutions and property rights, especially within national legal systems. See, for example, North (1990) and Hart (1995). For analysis of the effects of institutions on the success of efforts to manage common pool resources see, especially, Ostrom (1990). Political scientists and international lawyers, have done much to extend the analysis to the role of international insti-

tutions in governing international society. See, for example, Bull (1977); Krasner (1983); Keohane (1989); Young (1989b). For a recent and accessible review of the role of institutions (including various types of property rights) in managing common resources, see Ostrom et al. (1999).

8. In making this argument I draw, especially, on Slaughter's (1992, 1995) work on the "zone of law" that extends across the advanced liberal democracies.

9. On the influence of treaties, see Henkin (1979), Franck (1990), and Chayes and Chayes (1995). On legalization, see Abbott et al. (2000), in particular, and the summer 2000 issue of *International Organization* generally.

CHAPTER ONE
CRISIS AND OPPORTUNITY

1. Data from the U.S. Energy Information Administration show that since 1990 emissions are up 10% and growing at 1.2% per year (average since 1990), which would lead to a 27% increase above 1990 levels by 2010 (the midpoint of the 2008–2012 Kyoto budget period). Much has been made of the fact that data for 1998 show that U.S. emissions of carbon dioxide from the burning of fossil fuels (the main cause of global warming) rose by only 0.4% above 1997 levels, which may suggest that growth rates are slowing and perhaps it will be easier to comply with the Kyoto targets. For data that show the slight (0.4%) increase in fossil fuel carbon emissions from 1997 to 1998 although the economy grew by 3.9% (transportation emissions rose 1.8% but industrial emissions declined 1.2%), see Energy Information Administration (1999). For commentary on the world situation, based on data from BP Amoco, see Flavin (1999). One should not overinterpret data from one year since the phenomena that decouple economic growth from emissions—such as substitution of carbon-intensive coal by natural gas, and the shift from energy-intensive manufacturing to services—occur over many decades and are unlikely to accelerate sustainably in just one year. Indeed, the flagging growth in U.S. emissions for 1998 is, in large part, the consequence of warm winter temperatures rather than a sudden shift in technology. In my view, over the long term emissions will decouple almost fully from economic growth, and the future world will be

wealthy but greenhouse forcing will be much lower than the typical high-coal baseline scenarios that many models generate. [For a review of the literature, presentation of models, and elaboration of these points, see Grübler et al. (1999).] But the rate of decoupling—also known as "decarbonization"—is slow (about 0.25% per year for the U.S. economy over the last 100 years); over the short term, economic output is probably the main factor that affects emissions. The data discussed here are only for CO_2 from fossil fuel combustion; accounting rules in the Kyoto Protocol allow inclusion of other sources and sinks and may reduce the need for controls on CO_2, but probably not by much; that issue is discussed further below. Data from the U.S. Environmental Protection Agency (USEPA, 2000) show that trends in total emissions (11% higher than 1990 levels in 1998) are the same whether one examines just CO_2 from fossil fuel combustion or all greenhouse gases.

2. This figure is based on the Clinton Administration's analysis (see Clinton Administration, 1998). For an independent analysis using the same macroeconomic model (the "second generation model"), which arrives at compatible conclusions about permit prices and, by implication, costs, see MacCracken et al. (1999). There are about 100 million households in the United States, so the Administration's analysis translates into about $100 billion in annual cost. Other studies indicate similar losses from imposition of the Kyoto limits on the United States without allowing for trading. For example, Manne and Richels (1999) report a $90 billion per year annual loss in gross domestic product (GDP). For a review of cost estimates see Shogren (1999). For comparison, total spending on air and water programs was about $90 billion in 1994 [Council on Environmental Quality (CEQ), 1997]. The data series on pollution control expenditures was discontinued after 1994 and has been fraught with measurement problems; the comparison is intended only to indicate the order of magnitude. The costs of climate change are measured in welfare loss (e.g., loss in GDP), whereas the clean air and water program figures are expenditures, which are difficult to measure and do not necessarily fully represent losses to the economy.

3. In the Kyoto Protocol, see Article 17 (emission trading), Article 6 (JI), and Article 12 (CDM). Technically, a fourth type of trading is also allowed: the "bubble" (Article 4), which allows industrialized countries to pool their commitments and comply "jointly." That provision was created principally for the European Union (EU) whose member states

each have an identical commitment under the Protocol (8% cut in emissions); those formal commitments have been pooled across the EU and then reallocated. There is some legal controversy over whether and how other countries might create bubbles and whether such bubbles could, in effect, allow emission trading even if the rules required to implement the Article 17 emission trading system were not adopted. In this book I do not address the legal modalities of the "bubble" further; rather, my purpose is to look at the fundamental political and economic issues that surround trading.

4. See note 2 for more information about cost estimates.

5. See also the in-depth review of the five European climate programs by Gummer and Moreland (2000), which arrives at a similar conclusion.

6. For the outlines, see European Commission (2000).

7. Exactly how these investments would flow, and their magnitude, remains unclear. Already a few mutual funds for CDM investments are emerging, such as the World Bank's Prototype Carbon Fund, and various models for CDM schemes are under discussion. For an accessible and informative tutorial, see Baumert et al. (2000).

8. For the long list of outstanding issues related to trading, see Conference of the Parties (1998, decision 7/CP.4); the two-year timetable is not a legal deadline but a widely cited expectation based on the time needed—after 2000—for countries to ratify and implement the Protocol (Hogue, 1998). See also note 1 in Chapter 4.

9. For an inventory showing that all temperate and boreal forests are increasing in size and density, see UNECE/FAO (2000).

10. That figure is based on statistics from USEPA (2000); 14% is computed as the fraction of the most recent U.S. emissions (1998). The official U.S. position paper on accounting rules for CO_2 sinks (United States Government, 2000) suggests that the United States could earn credits of similar magnitude.

11. Some countries, including the United States, claim that it is possible to measure country-wide sinks accurately. However, that claim is not based on a serious analysis of the uncertainties. There are also some legal problems. Article 3.3 of the Kyoto Protocol states that only sinks "resulting from direct human-induced land-use change and forestry activities" can earn credit; at this writing (fall 2000) there is no agreed scheme for differentiating "direct" sinks from other factors that also cause trees to grow and sequester carbon (e.g., warmer climates and

higher CO_2 levels). Nor is it clear if trends such as rebounding of forests on abandoned agriculture lands, which long predate global warming policies, would qualify. Article 3.4, which concerns other land-use sinks (e.g., agricultural soils), suggests that credits could be deferred until the second budget period (i.e., after 2012); no decisions have been reached on how those credits would be measured or awarded. For the best summary of the issues that surround accounting rules for land use, see Schlamadinger and Marland (2000); for a comprehensive analysis see Watson et. al. (2000).

12. For a theoretical treatment and some application of data, see Jonas et al. (1999). To my knowledge, no other studies have quantified the "verification times" for carbon sinks.

13. Chapter 2 describes the calculations behind these numbers in more detail.

14. On this point, see especially Hahn and Stavins (1999). Countries may adopt various domestic measures other than trading at the national level—taxes, emission standards, technology programs, and the like. That is the scenario explored by Hahn and Stavins (1999), who argue that such diversity of national approaches is likely and that it does not lead to cost minimization, even if governments adopt an international permit trading system. That study is the only one of which I am aware that addresses this critical issue: the relationship between an international trading system and national policy measures. I subscribe to their view and draw an additional conclusion: every nation will probably need to adopt some form of national trading system, even if most of their national regulatory effort occurs through mechanisms other than trading. The need to meet a strict quantity target requires a mechanism for trading credits. Hence, for example, the European Union, which has long been officially skeptical of trading, is now developing a proposal for domestic and international trading that would complement other regulatory efforts by the EU and its member states (European Commission, 2000).

15. For the Berlin Mandate, see Conference of the Parties (1995, Decision 1/CP.1). For a dissenting view on targets and timetables prior to Berlin, see Victor and Salt (1995).

16. The literature on the lessons from the Montreal Protocol is extensive. The discussion here is my assessment of the proper lessons that

are centrally relevant to the architecture of a greenhouse gas regulatory system, derived mainly from analytical histories of the Protocol. For the main histories and analysis, see Benedick (1998), Parson (1993), Parson and Greene (1995), and Brack (1996). Since my focus here is the regulatory architecture and my point is only to illustrate the importance of architecture briefly with this important historical example, my discussion of the lessons from the ozone regime is of course not complete. For example, I do not discuss the importance of periodic scientific assessments, which were also a crucial element of the success of the Montreal Protocol (and are a central element of international efforts to regulate greenhouse gases, although the institutional arrangements differ).

17. The economic logic follows Weitzman (1974), as applied to the problem of climate change by Pizer (1999). For more detail, see chapter 4.

18. For the original logic in favor of setting prices and quantities, see Roberts and Spence (1976). For an initial application, see McKibbin and Wilcoxen (1997). This has also been labeled the "Resources for the Future (RFF) Proposal"; see Kopp (1999). As the system matured, governments might also set minimum prices and regulate the market in a manner similar to currency markets with managed floating rates—in currency markets central banks coordinate trading of reserves around agreed ranges of exchange rates, and in the carbon market the "carbon central bankers" might buy and sell permits to keep prices within agreed ranges. The more allowance is made for intervention in the market to control prices, the more the hybrid system will begin to resemble a pure tax approach.

19. Nonetheless, the hybrid approach does not eliminate problems of monitoring and enforcement. For example, rules may be needed that bar governments from using the proceeds from permit sales to offset the cost of carbon abatement, such as subsidies on the production and consumption of coal. Monitoring and enforcing such standards will be difficult. In the early stages, where permits are plentiful and target prices are low, such standards are probably not important—but work is needed so that standards and institutions for monitoring and enforcing them could be added to a hybrid system in the future.

20. Margolis and Kammen (1999); Morgan and Tierney (1998).

21. Dooley (1998).

22. PCAST (1997); SEAB (1995).

23. Other scholars and policy advocates have also called for increased investment in knowledge. See, in particular, Jacoby et al. (1998), Heinz Center (1999), PCAST (1997), and on the international dimensions PCAST (1999). I am completing a separate book that explores in detail how the U.S. government could craft and implement "technology policy" for global warming.

24. Keith and Dowlatabadi (1992).

25. Tenner (1996).

26. For more on quicker fixes with methane (and other short-lived radiatively active emissions, such as soot), see Hansen et al. (2000). In principle, Hansen et al. (2000) are right to emphasize that policy should include attention to all radiatively active emissions. In practice, however, CO_2 is still, by far, the most important emission. The Hansen et al. paper demonstrates that, but many news accounts of the paper have misunderstood the analysis and reported that Hansen et al. (2000) concluded that CO_2 need not be a central focus of global warming policy. Also, the Hansen et al. (2000) approach does not necessarily help much with the problem of complying with the Kyoto Protocol. Soot, for example, is not part of the Kyoto Protocol—no amount of sooty effort will have any impact on compliance with the Kyoto commitments.

27. Cook (1995); Victor and MacDonald (1999). In some countries the emission of these gases has already been cut sharply with little public intervention, which is indicative of the potential for further reductions.

28. In theory, the most appropriate approach would entail setting targets for the rate and absolute level of greenhouse warming over specific time periods, which would require that governments explicitly agree on the exact level of harm they could tolerate over different periods. From that agreement, targets for emission quantities (or, perhaps, prices) could then be derived. A proposal by the Government of Brazil (1997) envisioned such a system. At present it is probably technically too complicated to implement, not least because there is no agreed way to set the collective goals.

29. For critiques that abatement costs under the Kyoto Protocol far exceed the benefits of less warming, see especially Nordhaus and Boyer

(2000); for the argument that climate change and rising CO_2 concentrations may actually bring benefits, such as to farmers, see Mendelsohn (1999). For a critique that Kyoto empowers intrusive and undemocratic international institutions, see Rabkin (1998).

CHAPTER TWO
KYOTO'S FANTASYLAND

1. See, e.g., Schelling (1997); Cooper (1998).
2. Thus the Kyoto Protocol illustrates the general hypothesis of Young (1989a) on the formation of international regimes for governing shared resources: uncertainty makes it easier to negotiate an agreement because it obscures exactly who wins and loses.
3. Estimated value computed from the U.S. analysis (Clinton Administration, 1998) and similar results presented by MacCracken et al. (1999) based on the same economic model but with more transparent assumptions.
4. For the Decision, see Conference of the Parties (1996, Decision 9/CP.2); for more information on the methodology for adjusting base years, see Victor et al. (2000).
5. Nakićenović et al. (1998).
6. For the IIASA/WEC study see Nakićenović et al. (1998); for the calculation of carbon emissions shown in figure 2.1, see Victor et al. (2000). The shaded boxes show the difference between the Kyoto targets and the "middle course (B)" scenario, which is in the middle of the IIASA/WEC range of scenarios and assumes that countries do not implement policies to regulate emissions. In other words, it is a "business as usual" scenario, but with lower consumption of coal than is typical of the baseline scenario of the Intergovernmental Panel on Climate Change (known as the IPCC/IS92a scenario). The range in estimated transfers to Russia and Ukraine reflects a wide range of permit prices, which in turn is a function of different assumptions about Western demand for permits. See Victor et al. (2000) for details. The estimated transfers are based on five years only, not the full asset price, because it is unlikely that Russia and Ukraine will be given these windfall assets into perpetuity. However, depending on how the trading rules are developed and the politics of subsequent permit allocations evolve,

leasing could allow them to raise similar revenue without an outright sale of the asset.

7. Albright (1998).

8. United States Senate (1997, 1998); see also Byrd and Hagel (1998).

9. Eizenstat and Loy (1998).

10. There are serious unresolved legal questions about whether binding commitments would make a country eligible for Annex B status and thus eligible for trading. Kazakhstan has made a formal proposal to amend the FCCC to add its name to Annex I (see Climate Change Secretariat, 1999). If successful, that effort would open the path to adding Kazakhstan to Annex B of the Kyoto Protocol; in turn, that might allow a target for Kazakhstan that includes a windfall similar to the one granted to Russia and Ukraine. For now, Kazakhstan has suspended its formal effort to change Annex B because the international negotiations already have too many other issues on the agenda. Argentina, in contrast, is working (with substantial technical assistance from the United States) to develop a plan and target. (I doubt those efforts will bear much fruit—unless it is a target that is heavily padded with a windfall—because there is little public support in Argentina for spending resources to slow global warming.) It would be much more difficult legally for Argentina to join Annex B of the Kyoto Protocol and thus be eligible for trading. However, by adopting a nationwide target (liberally padded with headroom), Argentina may be able to ease the process of earning credits through the CDM and, in effect, enter the trading system. In countries that adopt a binding cap for their total emissions it may not be necessary to determine the particular emission reductions due to each CDM project. The transaction costs of the CDM would be much lower, and it would operate more like a pure trading system.

11. This general problem of negotiating contracts under conditions of uncertainty is a frequent topic in research on game theory and contracting. In international law, one strategy for addressing this problem is to negotiate "soft" agreements that have a low level of legal obligation, low specificity, and/or weak procedures for dispute resolution. In the case of emission trading, however, the "soft" route is not available because the trading system requires high levels of confidence in the security of the property rights—it must be clear who owns how many permits. Codification of trading systems must occur with "hard" inter-

national law—binding treaties with high specificity and strong enforcement. Hard law especially produces the dynamics that I discuss in the
main text—reluctant participants that are wary of uncertainty and focused on the worst-case scenario. For a review and applications of
"hard" and "soft" concepts to international legal contracting issues, see
Abbott and Snidal (2000). For an exploration of the role of uncertainty
in contracting, see Hart (1995).

12. For the most complete argument along these lines, see Wiener
(1999).

13. Grubb (1988).

14. On the argument for fairness, which attributes an even stronger
role to fairness than the "all else equal" weaker version that I present here, see Franck (1990, 1995). For a counterargument that argues
that it is willingness to pay, rather than fairness, that principally explains successful international environmental cooperation, see Victor
(1998b).

15. Some observers may object to this statement because there are
many projects under way through the pilot phase for "'activities implemented jointly (AIJ)" under the Framework Convention on Climate
Change. (For a list, see http://www.unfccc.int/program/aij.) These projects, along with many others that are not officially classified as AIJ pilot
phase projects, could be incorporated into the CDM, once the CDM is
officially launched. Moreover, I am mindful of the most important single development, so far, in the evolution of the CDM: creation, by the
World Bank, of the Prototype Carbon Fund (PCF, described at www.
PrototypeCarbonFund.org). The PCF pools resources from governments and firms (totaling about $135 million in fall 2000) to invest in
projects. Pooling helps to lower transaction costs and increases the
chance that important lessons learned from one project will be applied
to others. These are, indeed, important developments, and in this book
I argue that the CDM is an important innovation that should be preserved. But the issue is whether transaction costs can be reduced to
a sufficiently low level and whether baselines can be sufficiently well
determined that the CDM can become an extremely active and efficient
mechanism for a wide range of projects. On those points, I am pessi-
mistic, and the current experience with the AIJ pilot phase and with
earlier "baseline and credit" trading schemes (see note 16) supports that
pessimism.

16. For more on CDM-like trading programs under the 1977 Clean Air Act Amendments in the United States, see Hahn and Hester (1989). For more analysis of trading of emission reduction credits in the Los Angeles basin, with emphasis on the effects of transaction costs and intervention by regulators, see Foster and Hahn (1995). For an initial assessment of some projects from the AIJ pilot phase, which underscores the difficulty of measuring how far a project has reduced emissions below the baseline (the so-called "additionality" problem), see Beuermann et al. (2000). For assessment of the U.S. pilot program on JI and the severe effects of extensive bureaucratic review, see Lile et al. (1998).

17. On the "industrial flight" hypothesis and evidence from the real world, see Leonard (1988), Low (1992), Vogel (1995), and World Bank (2000). The hypothesis appears to hold when the cost differential is large and markets are especially sensitive to price—e.g., in production of resource-intensive commodities. Thus, in the case of global warming industrial flight might be concentrated in mining, smelting, and other energy-intensive activities. But many other uses of energy are intertwined with other economic activities for which flight is much less likely. The problem of flight can be overcome through compensation— as I discuss in the main text of this study—but if, in practice, flight is concentrated in a few sectors it might be more efficient (and politically more effective) to concentrate compensation in the affected sectors at home rather than compensating whole countries abroad to join the agreement. That is, wag the tail, not the dog. In some cases, such domestic compensation schemes would be incompatible with WTO rules on subsidies. Some, like Rabkin (1998), argue that this is not worth the risk of complicating and undermining the WTO. Hence, as I will argue below, the only way to stem leakage is at the source and in a manner that is embedded in the WTO rather than from an imperfect distance. I do not further address the economic costs and modeling of leakage— this note of diversion is simply to point out that the debate on "industrial flight" was remarkably similar to the debate on leakage, yet many people have forgotten that many of the feared forms of industrial flight never came to pass because, in the real world, markets are stickier and more sensitive to a wider range of factors than in the friction-free world that typically exists inside the models that are used to assess the level of leakage.

18. See the ruling in WTO Appellate Body (1998).

19. See, for example, the partially successful attempts by reluctant parties to weaken the Montreal Protocol's Non-Compliance Procedure (Victor, 1998a).

20. For a study showing that enforcement and leakage are two aspects of the same problem, see Barrett (1998). For an argument in favor of "broad then deep," see Schmalensee (1998). For a critique that emphasizes the weakness of learning from broad and shallow agreements, and the problems of gaining developing countries' participation even for shallow commitments, see Hahn (1998, p. 39).

21. In the words of Slaughter (1992), these nations are already in the "zone of law." Or, in the words of Chayes and Chayes (1995), they have accepted that the "new sovereignty" requires participating in demanding international regimes. But see Rabkin's (1998) warning on the need for constitutional protections against intrusive and unelected international bureaucracies.

22. The literature on the sulfur program is extensive and growing. See, in particular, Schmalensee et al. (1998), Joskow et al. (1998), and Stavins (1998). See also data and reports from the EPA Acid Rain program at http://www.epa.gov/docs/acidrain. Once there was broad agreement that regulation of acid-causing emissions was necessary, the political bargaining process over how to allocate permits ("allowances") during the two phases as well as the size and allocation of compensation to affected mining interests was extremely detailed. Here I indicate only the highlights of the story. For an attempt at quantitative analysis of the influences and outcomes, see especially Joskow and Schmalensee (1998). One indication that the Kyoto negotiators were unaware of the magnitude of the assets that they were allocating is how quickly and superficially the two-month final stages of Kyoto negotiations proceeded, in contrast with the longer and much more detailed wrangling over the allocations in the creation of the U.S. sulfur trading program.

23. For more on the weak and conservative nature of international law, see Henkin (1979, chapter 1). For more on the implications of unit-veto rules that are commonplace in international law (and how to make agreements more effective in light of them), see Victor (1997) and Wiener (1999). Wiener concludes that, because it provides each party incentive to join the international agreement, there is a presumption in favor of emission trading. Because permits can be used for compensa-

tion, he argues, it is easier to entice reluctant parties. My view is that this conclusion probably holds only under restrictive conditions—such as the existence of perfect information on preferences and costs and the lack of moral hazard—that do not exist in the real world of global warming policy. Moreover, parties will soon learn that compensation is a zero-sum game and the efforts to entice reluctant parties will thus soon deteriorate into difficult zero-sum bargaining—thus, in reality, permits will have no special advantage over the alternatives and are probably much worse. See the discussion below for more detail.

24. Wigley et al. (1996). For simplicity I will not elaborate the full argument here. One caveat is particularly important: the "wait then abate" strategy is not effective if waiting entails simply biding time while hoping for a technological breakthrough. Investments in new technology are needed, and thus some abatement may be justified if it results in such technological investments. See Grübler et al. (1999) for additional detail with results from models that employ learning curves—such models yield low-cost energy technologies only when investments are made.

25. All exchanges (U.S. and overseas) for domestically listed companies. Data for 31 January 2000 at http://www.nyse/com/marketinfo/marketcapitalization.html

26. Gates (1968).

27. "Bids for new U.K. mobile franchises soar past $16bn," *Financial Times*, 1–2 April 2000, p. 1.

28. For more on the politics of limiting hot air transfers, see Grubb et al. (1999). The European Union has sought to limit trading not only through the use of caps but also with other proposed rules, such as the requirement to hold large amounts of permits in reserve accounts, subject to final determination that the seller is in compliance.

CHAPTER THREE
MONITORING AND ENFORCEMENT

1. This range includes the $14 per ton estimate used to calculate the figures in table 2.1; see the caption for more information.

2. Chayes and Chayes (1995). Similar arguments are repeated in Brown Weiss and Jacobson (1998). See also Franck (1990).

3. An often cited quote from this school is from Henkin (1979, p. 47): "almost all nations observe almost all principles of international

law and almost all of their obligations almost all of the time." But Henkin knew (indeed stated in chapter 1) that international law is conservative and weak—poor at changing the status quo when change is costly.

4. Raustiala and Victor (1998).

5. Downs et al. (1996); Victor (1997); Victor et al. (1998).

6. GAO (1992); Ausubel and Victor (1992).

7. Sand (1997); Lanchbery (1998).

8. This assertion is based on interviews with people who work with the data sets as well as on my attempts to match import and export certificates using available data. The assertion cannot be proved because, the data on the universe of violations do not exist—suspected violations are, by definition, not proven. For more on the sources of the data in the NGO network (in particular, the TRAFFIC network) and the process for formally lodging and addressing infractions, see Sand (1997).

9. For example, data reported by Russia and by Lebanon. See the discussion in the chapters on the Montreal Protocol by Victor and by Greene in Victor et al. (1998).

10. Neue and Boonjawat (1998), table 8.1. Every new study that I see confirms the high variability of rice-related methane emissions. For a recent study on methane from rice in China, for example, see Cai et al. (2000).

11. See the review in Neue and Boonjawat (1998); see also the review of mitigation potentials in Mosier et al. (1998), which suggests that methane emissions could be cut in half by changes in irrigation technique.

12. See Victor (1991a).

13. On oil pollution and tankers, see Mitchell (1994).

14. UNECE/FAO (2000).

15. For comparison of different inventories, see Shvidenko and Nilsson (1998) and also Nilsson et al. (2000).

16. Schimel et al. (2000). "Uncertainty" here is the difference between the fluxes reported by Schimel et al. (2000) and those reported by U.S. national inventories. The two numbers are not completely comparable; however, the purpose of the comparison is to illustrate the range of possible uncertainty, not to give an exact number. For worries about uncertainty in and monitoring of carbon stocks on agriculture and grazing lands, see Subak (2000).

17. The literature that demonstrates the complexity of accounting for carbon fluxes from land-use changes is extensive. For a recent study, with a brief review of some mechanisms and relevant literature, see Schlesinger (1999). For a study that underscores the difficulty of identifying the net flux from the gross flux, using the example of Russia, see Nilsson et al. (2000). For a study showing the enormous effect of different accounting rules on the estimated carbon fluxes from forests, see Liski et al. (2000). For one of many studies showing the difficulty of monitoring carbon sequestration from projects that are typical of the types of projects that might be favored under the Kyoto Protocol, see Pinard and Putz (1997).

18. For a theoretical study on verification times, see Jonas et al. (1999). For an application to carbon accounting in Russia, see Nilsson et al. (2000).

19. For example, Hayhoe et al. (1999) and especially Reilly et al. (1999). Both these studies make use of the methane abatement costs in EPA (1998), which shows why the argument for a multigas approach must be mathematically true—the marginal cost of regulating methane is lower than for many projects that regulate CO_2 only. The same is true of projects to cut perfluorocarbons and sulfur hexafluoride, for which marginal costs for many abatement activities are negative (Victor and MacDonald, 1999).

20. See Dudek and Wiener (1996) and Lile et al. (1998).

21. For the original statement of this policy, known as the "comprehensive approach," see Department of Justice (1990). For a critique, which emerged from a study financed by the EPA, see Victor (1991a).

22. For example, as Reilly et al. (1999) show, there is little difference between a CO_2-only and a multigas approach for modest cuts in emissions (e.g., the Kyoto Protocol), but the lower cost of a multigas approach becomes apparent as the regulatory effort tightens.

23. This statement, though widely believed, may not be rigorously true—other Annex I countries may, also, have had positive net land use emissions in 1990. This possibility is an illustration of both the fact that more work is needed to improve inventories and also the fact that the numbers are probably soft enough that nations can tune their inventories to their advantage. See, e.g., a report on the U.K. inventory which suggests a net flux of carbon to the atmosphere in 1990 from the U.K. terrestrial carbon system (Cannell et al., 1999).

24. Hamilton and Vellen (1999).

25. On human rights, see Farer and Gaer (1993).

26. Author's assessment, based on review of dispute resolution procedures in all major multilateral environmental agreements. From that set I exclude trade agreements that have had environmental issues grafted onto them—in particular, the North American Free Trade Agreement (NAFTA), for which the "teeth" of the dispute resolution mechanism are still unclear. Environmental disputes have also been handled in the World Trade Organization and the General Agreement on Tariffs and Trade (Charnovitz, 1998). I also exclude bilateral agreements (e.g., under the International Joint Commission) and the multilateral agreements of the European Union and associated regional partnerships, which are stronger because the core political integration is also stronger. This review is not to assert that it is impossible to create strong dispute resolution procedures—clearly that is wrong. Indeed, a few regimes for managing international resources have created dispute resolution procedures that could, in practice, be powerful either by themselves or in conjunction with other dispute resolution procedures available under international law. For example, in a dispute concerning whether Japan was overfishing the stock of bluefin tuna for sashimi, Australia and New Zealand argued that the compulsory dispute resolution procedures of the United Nations Convention on the Law of the Sea could be applied, and through those procedures on 27 August 1999 they obtained a temporary injunction against a Japanese tuna fishing program. One year later, however, that injunction was overturned when an international tribunal argued that the dispute resolution procedures of the 1993 Convention for the Conservation of Southern Bluefin Tuna, which applied specifically to the stock of tuna in question, prohibited compulsory settlement of disputes (see Schiffman, 1999, on the dispute and Schwebel et al., 2000, for the arbitral decision overturning the injunction). This partial exception helps prove the rule—it is difficult to get parties to agree to strong dispute resolution mechanisms in the types of agreements that have been used as models for the Framework Convention and the Kyoto Protocol. In the fall of 2000, as I am completing this book, negotiators are developing a compliance mechanism for the Framework Convention and Kyoto Protocol that may help to offset the tendency for formal dispute resolution procedures to be stillborn or weak. I resist speculating on the strength of this compliance mecha-

nism, however, because efforts to negotiate compliance mechanisms in other environmental accords have often produced strong visions during the negotiations with much of the strength eliminated when the text is finally adopted and implemented.

27. Birnie and Boyle (1992). See my caveat about the bluefin tuna case in note 26.

28. On the Montreal Protocol's noncompliance procedure, see Victor (1998a). Generally on lessons learned from noncompliance procedures and similar mechanisms, see Wiser (1999).

29. Charnovitz (1994).

30. On the general use of sanctions, see Hufbauer et al. (1990). Because unilateral sanctions are rarely effective, coalitions are needed; on the difficulty of mobilizing sanctioning coalitions, see Martin (1992).

31. For a theoretical treatment, see Downing and Brady (1981); for an application to enforcement of multilateral environmental agreements, see also the review in Victor et al. (1998, pp. 305–326), Raustiala and Victor (1998), and Victor and Skolnikoff (1999).

32. Olson (1965) warned that forming groups for collective action is difficult when the benefits of action are diffuse. Existing organizations, such as the International Chamber of Commerce, might make collective action easier to organize and offset some of the Olsonian pessimism, but the basic insight holds—the benefits of tight enforcement are diffuse.

33. On the importance of the zone of law and its effect on preferences, rule of law, trade, and other interactions, see Slaughter (1992, 1995) and Moravcsik (1997). For an application to international environmental cooperation, see Raustiala and Victor (1998).

34. The assumption is so widely held that it has not been subjected to much detailed analysis. For statements in favor of seller liability, see, for example, the analysis by Toman summarized in *International Environment Reporter* (1998) and also the analysis by Kerr (1998). Both Toman and Kerr argue that transaction costs in a buyer liability system will be excessive. Both rightly suggest that buyer liability should be the norm for CDM trading, which I do not address here.

35. Some will claim that reputation effects will deter a party from actions that merit expulsion. Buyers will be located mainly in the advanced industrialized countries and may fear public retribution if they engage in shady permit purchases. Buyers and sellers may also want

to establish good reputations because they think that will ease future transactions. But reputation effects play little role when liability rules impose a cost on the seller alone for deviant behavior and when all permits are comingled identically in a single world market.

36. Some problems of seller liability might be reduced if the scheme allowed for some differentiation of sellers—for example, a rating system. But doing that would require agreement on an intergovernmental framework and rating institutions; yet, as discussed earlier, international institutions are weak and lack freedom of action, and it is often difficult to gain agreement for international enforcement procedures and actions. Private markets, driven by buyer liability, have demonstrated that they can probably better provide these ratings to address risk. Even in international finance—where institutions are much more advanced than in environmental diplomacy—it has proved to be very difficult to gain intergovernmental agreement on sensible categories for banking risks. Witness the difficulties in revising the banking standards in the Basle accord, which now include risk categories that most experts do not think are well connected to the actual banking system risks.

37. Observers of the Kyoto scene will recognize that the liability proposals under debate are a lot more complicated than the discussion that I have presented here; however, the fundamentals are identical. At present, there appears to be a a consensus developing in favor of a "compliance period reserve" that would put some permits into a holding account somewhat akin to an escrow system. A requirement for only a small reserve account with rapid release would operate somewhat akin to seller liability. Moreover, there are many other proposals for allocating liability that are variants on the fundamental approaches considered here. They include, for example, a "traffic light" system—green, yellow, red—proposed in a thoughtful paper by Goldberg et al. (1998). When the green light is on, seller liability rules. Liability shifts to buyers when risks of noncompliance are significant (yellow). A red light might stop trading or impose full buyer liability. Institutionally, such a system must be designed for its most onerous purpose, and thus in practice it requires the permit tracking institutions and costs of a buyer liability system. When the green light is on, the system offers the assurance to purchasers that a seller liability system provides, but the same is true of a buyer liability system that is covered by insurance and/or when buyers purchase from reputable sellers. Thus the key question is when and how

the light shifts from green to yellow. A continuous gradation of color—in effect, buyer liability—where markets rather than bureaucrats assess the risks, would be more efficient. For a recent study that, like the stoplight system, proposes shifting liability, see Nordhaus et al. (2000). Several analysts speak of "shared liability" in which both buyers and settlers have accountability. In my view, such systems are, in essence, buyer liability mechanisms and are only as strong as their buyer liability rules. Finally, I note that the literature on liability rules uses term "seller liability" loosely. In practice, each seller may not be held liable but, rather, the original issuer of permits (a nation) may be liable for behavior within its jurisdiction.

38. This idea is based on an optimal enforcement strategy—which focuses monitoring activity based on past performance—described by Russell et al. (1986).

Chapter Four
Rethinking the Architecture

1. There is no single date that is the point of no return for Kyoto, in part because the date varies with a country's system for regulating economic activity. In the United States, a clear decision to pursue ratification of the Kyoto Protocol—which is unlikely to occur until after the 2000 presidential election, if at all—would require perhaps six months to one year for the development of implementing legislation, which must accompany the formal decision (by the U.S. Senate) to ratify the protocol. If one allows for some additional delays—which is not unreasonable given the opposition to the protocol that already exists and the fact that many analysts expect substantial economic effects from adopting the protocol, which will engender further scrutiny—then perhaps a total of three years would be needed from the decision to pursue ratification to the entry into force of appropriate legislation (and other rules). Counting backwards from 1 January 2008, the deadline is the end of 2004. However, unless firms can comply overnight—which is impossible unless they will be able to meet essentially all of their obligations by purchasing permits overseas or through easy low-cost actions—some additional time will be needed for cost-effective measures to be put into place. How much time is needed is a hotly contested issue, depending mainly on whether one thinks that there are large op-

portunities for quickly achieving emission abatement at low cost, such as through simple changes in production processes or minor behavioral changes that reduce energy consumption. Alternatively, if abatement will require more elaborate changes to the capital stock, it will be very costly unless abatement measures are put into place along with the turnover of the capital stock, which varies from a few years (appliances) to several decades (power plants). In short, the point of no return is a function of cost. My guess is that, for targets of the magnitude of the Kyoto Protocol, the costs will rise dramatically if the time allowed between sending a clear signal to firms that they must meet emission targets and the date when those targets take effect is less than about five years. For targets that are stricter than the Kyoto limits—or if trading were limited, which would have an effect on firms similar to the imposition of stricter targets—the needed advance time may be as high as a few decades, which is the average lifetime of the energy-relevant capital stock. The point at which firms receive a clear signal is perhaps near the midpoint of the three-year political process between the decision to take Kyoto seriously and the actual implementation of legislation. That means that a formal decision to pursue Kyoto is needed about 6.5 years prior to the onset of the Kyoto limits (i.e., approximately the middle of 2001).

2. The main story in research on the effects of climate change on agriculture and coastal zones is that the impacts shrink dramatically when allowance is made for humans' ability to adapt. For a brief review of research on agriculture impacts that emphasizes the importance of adaptation, see Mendelsohn (1999). For a review of the impacts of rising sea levels with similar emphasis, see Yohe et al. (2000).

3. See Schelling (1997). On the argument that higher incomes improve the capacity of individuals and societies to adapt, see Wildavsky (1980). On adaptive capacity, see also Schelling (1983), Kates et al. (1985), and Ausubel (1991).

4. For this scenario, see Still et al. (1999).

5. For example, Broecker (1987), Stocker and Schmittner (1998), and Wood et al. (1999).

6. Cooper (1998, 1999).

7. The basic logic is in Weitzman (1974); for a cogent application to climate change, see especially Pizer (1999).

8. Note that the Kyoto Protocol emission trading system averages over five years rather than requiring that a quantity limit be met every year, which reduces the risk that the economy will be forced to make especially rapid and short-term reductions in greenhouse gas emissions. However, no study has rigorously examined whether five years is the right period for averaging. A system for "early action" credits, which has been proposed in the United States and a few other countries, could also help stretch the period for meeting a quantity cap over time and reduce the risk that the economy will be forced to reduce emissions rapidly. But "early action" has an uncertain political future and will have little impact on behavior if firms expect that the protocol's emission limits will be rejected in the United States. For an early partial application of the Weitzman (1974) logic to the climate problem see Epstein and Gupta (1990). Their analysis concludes that an emission trading program is superior to the alternatives (including taxation) because trading would allow firms to hedge risks, which Epstein and Gupta think is not an attribute of tax-based approaches. In my view, that analysis is incorrect and the certainty of cost from a price mechanism is better for firms than hedging under a trading system. I note, however, that Epstein and Gupta underscore that their analysis was incomplete; among the issues that they did not consider were the allocation of permits, monitoring, and enforcement—the central issues of this book. Nor did they fully consider the potential costs to the economy if emission caps were set at levels so tight that they forced entire economies to implement crash reduction programs. Single firms can hedge against future risks, but it is harder for entire economies to do so (see note 9). I point out their study only to emphasize that it was one of the first to weigh different regimes; sadly, the debate quickly focused on trading and the analytical community increasingly ignored the alternatives.

9. In principle, as Epstein and Gupta (1990) argue (see note 8), a trading system could also facilitate long-term planning by allowing firms to purchase permits (or derivatives) to cover future emissions. One argument against this is the one I make in the main text—that investors gain the greatest information about future costs from a price instrument because that sets prices directly (rather than indirectly, through the permit market). The other argument I entertain only here in the notes. There are political attributes of a permit system that make it likely that all or most governments would adopt policies that result

in similar errors—higher emissions than expected and therefore lower availability of permits to cover new investments. These correlated errors, in turn, would trigger correlated (and unexpectedly high) economic costs. For evidence, consider the current debate about ratification and implementation of the Kyoto Protocol. No government knows exactly the efficacy of the policies that it and other governments are implementing to control emissions. But most governments want to make the Kyoto Protocol look feasible so that the public accepts the cost and legislatures will ratify the deal. The result is a danger that possible emissions during the years 2008 to 2012 will be systematically understated while claims for the ability to control emissions through low-cost policies are systematically overstated. In addition to understating future emissions, most western countries have found that planned policies to control emissions are often less effective than hoped. Some have failed entirely (e.g., the proposed carbon/energy tax in the European Union, which environment ministers invented and finance ministers scuttled). Only a few small countries have actually put any significant policies to control carbon into place (e.g., carbon taxes in Norway and Sweden); several countries are planning to implement new measures (e.g., the U.K. climate change levy). But most of these levies include exceptions that limit tax levels for high emitters and blunt the levy's practical effect on emissions. Moreover, these levies do not fix the quantity of emissions and thus create the risk that if most countries' measures are less effective than expected the quantity of emissions in each country will be higher than planned.

10. For a study focused in particular on how inclusion of a nasty "threshold" consequence affects the time path of emissions, see Keller et al. (2000). That study shows that threshold effects significantly increase the optimal amount of abatement; however, the exact change in optimal abatement level is significantly affected by the sensitivity of climate to the increase in greenhouse gases, which is a critical yet quite uncertain parameter in climate models. Thus the main conclusion to be drawn is that the optimal path of emission controls becomes more stringent than when such "threshold" effects are ignored but that it is still not possible to calculate a single threshold to be avoided. For more on the impact of possible catastrophic change on the optimal path for controlling emissions of greenhouse gases, see Lempert and Schlesinger (2000), which illustrates an important line of research that has sought

to identify policies that are "robust" with respect to many potential (yet uncertain) effects of climate change. Typically those policies include investments to improve the capacity to monitor climate changes, to lower the cost of future abatement of greenhouse gases, to begin undertaking some abatement now, and to promote adaptation. This approach is consistent with the one advocated in this book, although my focus is on the design of an international architecture for coordinating the effort to limit greenhouse gas emissions.

11. In particular, research that shows that tax measures are much more efficient than cap and trade systems—e.g., see Pizer (1999).

12. For example, a recent study by Hjoellund and Tinggaard (reported in Allen, 1999) shows that in each of the five European countries they examined (Denmark, Finland, the Netherlands, Norway, and Sweden) the carbon tax on industrial operations was on average four times lower than the tax on households. Industry, they argue, is better able to organize against the taxes than are households, and thus the effect of tax measures on industry is much smaller.

13. For a more detailed discussion of compliance with international environmental law and the factors that explain high compliance levels, see Victor et al. (1998) and Victor (1999).

14. WTO Appellate Body (1998).

15. Keesing (1998).

16. "The Changing Atmosphere: Implications for Global Security," July 1988, Toronto, Canada.

17. This opacity would free governments to follow Young's (1989a) advice—that agreement is easier to reach when stakes are unclear—without taking the advice to the extreme end and pursuing commitments without regard for level and allocation of cost.

18. Schelling (1997, 1998).

19. Victor (1991b).

20. I think the "round" approach has now reached the end of its useful life in the GATT/WTO system because the rounds have been so successful that they now take on an increasingly complex array of issues. Those include highly politicized topics (e.g., food safety and environmental standards) that used to be the province of purely domestic policy. Linking all these issues together into a single "round" makes it difficult to finish the round in a timely way (or even get it started),

and political dissent on one topic can easily sink the whole ship. Sector-specific agreements would be more effective, and thus the current effort to start a new "millennium round" is probably misplaced (Victor, 2000). However, for the climate issue, on which international coordination efforts are at the earliest stages, the "round" approach offers an effective device for linking issues.

21. See Hahn (1998).

22. Generally, governments are already thinking about complementarities between market-based measures and traditional regulation. This is especially important in Europe, where efforts to implement the Kyoto Protocol have revealed that some form of trading is probably essential to make it possible to meet the emission quantity targets exactly. However, most efforts to date in Europe to control emissions have focused on nonquantity measures, such as traditional regulation (e.g., emission standards) and taxation. For a thoughtful exploration of the synergies see EC (2000); see also Yamin and Lefevre (2000). Note that the relationships are not only synergies. A particular problem, for example, is that auto manufacturers appear to believe that they have been exempted from additional climate-related regulation by adopting "voluntary" measures to improve efficiency of new vehicles. (On the voluntary standards, see International Environment Reporter, 2000.) However, it is unclear whether and how automobiles could be excluded from a trading system.

23. For current information on EU and member country proposals see http://europa.eu.int/comm/environment/climat/home_en.htm.

24. On decarbonization see Nakićenović (1997) and Grübler et al. (1999).

25. For example, see the model runs cited by Grübler et al. (1999) and the logic for R&D investments outlined in Schneider and Goulder (1997).

26. For example, technological change is the single most important variable for explaining the wide variance in scenarios for future emissions of CO_2. For a review of scenarios that compares the effect of different factors on estimated emissions, see Nakićenović et al. (1999).

27. For example, Cohen and Noll (1991).

28. This approach is based on Roberts and Spence (1976), which McKibbin and Wilcoxen (1997) applied to the issue of global warming. See also Kopp (1999), which applies the hybrid approach to the Kyoto

Protocol by arguing that the compliance mechanism (Article 18) of the protocol should consist of a tax on excess emissions. One problem in transforming the Kyoto Protocol into such a system—which generally I favor—is that Article 18 requires that the protocol be amended if governments want to adopt a compliance mechanism that has "binding" consequences. As the whole point of the hybrid approach is that the tax would be binding, this idea for bringing taxes into the Kyoto Protocol through the back door in fact would require reopening the protocol for amendment—rebuilding the protocol, rather than merely modifying it.

29. For more on the importance of regulatory review in affecting the cost of project-by-project trading systems, see main text at chapter 2, note 16.

30. Conversely, nations might adopt stringent commitments and expect to have novel mechanisms at their disposal to help lower the cost of compliance. Indeed, that is the situation for the United States under the Kyoto Protocol—a significant part of the low-cost estimates for the United States depends upon the availability of a smoothly functioning CDM. The danger, however, is that the assumption that the CDM will operate smoothly—which I have argued is unlikely in practice—gives strong incentives to corrupt the system by adopting rules that make it excessively easy to earn CDM credits. That, too, is bad news for the CDM since excessive rewards will attract political opposition and demands for more cumbersome review procedures. For more on the role of the CDM in the U.S. cost estimates see note 2. Be mindful that the Clinton Administration's analysis is not transparent about its assumptions for transaction costs of the CDM. However, the MacCracken et al. (1999) study is, and it suggests that the only way the Clinton Administration could arrive at its low-cost compliance estimates is by assuming that the CDM is perfectly efficient. That scenario is as likely as snow in July in Washington.

31. Most of the controversy is, properly, about the fact that the surplus is a windfall—it is not the consequence of any effort to control emissions, and thus purchases of the windfall permits result in emissions that are higher than they would otherwise have been. In principle, large international economic flows may cause no economic harm; that may not be true if they flow from economies that use capital efficiently to those where corrupt or incompetent economic actors squander capital. In that situation, trading could exacerbate the economic cost of

efforts to regulate emissions of greenhouse gases, and the benefit of a scheme that would make it possible to limit international flows, such as the one outlined here, could be substantial.

32. For simplicity of exposition, I ignore here the effect of existing and new distortions within each participating economy (e.g., fossil fuel subsidies) that could make the effective marginal cost of greenhouse gas emissions vary, even if the nominal price of emission permits were identical.

33. In each round of allocation it might be possible to award additional permits to reluctant participants, which in effect would allow differentiation of costs. But after the first round it will be clear that that approach is simply printing money. I have addressed this issue already in my discussion of compensation in chapter 2—it is intriguing in theory but tricky to implement in practice. Another solution to the political problem caused as prices converge in a free permit market would be to devise a scheme of border adjustments that would allow nations to preserve different cost levels. But that would be tricky to design and difficult to square with international trade laws. Worse, adjusting permit prices at borders might undermine the central purpose of a trading system, which is to encourage firms to invest in the least costly controls on emissions.

34. Throughout this discussion I have addressed the "hybrid architecture" with the assumption that both the price and the quantity aspects of the system would be active. That is, large numbers of permits would be in circulation and governments would also sell significant numbers of new permits. Both these conditions are important since they allow the hybrid system to avoid the pitfalls of the textbook quantity or textbook price systems. For example, the existence of an active market in permit trading is necessary for discovery of the real price of carbon emissions, which in turn is essential to making it much easier to monitor compliance under the hybrid approach than under an architecture based on coordinated taxes. If diplomats were to allocate few permits and rely extensively on the sale of permits then the system would take on more of the attributes of the textbook tax system. In contrast, if diplomats set the agreed price too high then, in effect, they would have created a textbook trading system—and the pitfalls of allocation would emerge. It is beyond the scope of this book to explore what com-

binations of price and quantity cause the hybrid to take on excessive characteristics of one of its textbook parents.

35. See Hahn and Stavins (1999).

36. See, e.g., Rabkin (1998). I have not explored in detail the complementary rules and enforcement procedures that would be required to keep governments from merely substituting subsidies and other policies, blunting the effect of the agreed tax (in a tax system) or the agreed price cap (in a hybrid system). Some of those rules and enforcement procedures may be quite intrusive, although they are not radically more intrusive than constraints in the WTO on patent, competition, food safety, and other policy areas. I have suggested that the need for such complementary rules and enforcement procedures would be greatest, and most difficult to implement, in the "coordinated tax" and "policies and measures" architectures.

CHAPTER FIVE
AFTER KYOTO: WHAT NEXT?

1. If measurement errors were randomly and symmetrically distributed around a mean value then, on average, there would be no need for a penalty—some emissions would be underestimated, but an equal number would be overestimated, and thus the mean emission factors could be used. However, the need for a penalty arises when there is an incentive to misreport emissions and thus it is no longer valid to assume that errors are random and symmetrical.

2. This is a common problem in international environmental regimes—the problem of low data supply, a major concern until the early 1990s (e.g., GAO, 1992), is being solved through more attention to data reporting, but the problem of data quality is now more evident (see Raustiala and Victor, 1998). The problems have not been solved even where data reporting involves mainly high-income countries where international institutional capacity is high—for example, the European Environment Agency, which collects environmental data for the EU, is plagued by the low comparability of the data that member states report (see International Environment Reporter, 1996).

3. In-depth reviews (IDRs) have been conducted only for Annex I nations and include advanced industrial democracies as well as less

transparent nations (e.g., Russia). The starting point for the reviews is the submission of a "national communication"; only recently have developing countries begun to submit such communications, and it remains unclear what form, if any, in-depth reviews in the developing countries will take. Since the developing countries do not have regulatory obligations, some analysts think there is little need for them to undergo IDRs in the future. However, the point is that the process of submitting communications and undergoing IDRs could lay a foundation of knowledge and experience that would make it easier to negotiate sensible commitments in the future. That, exactly, is why many developing countries are wary of the process—it is, in their eyes, a slippery slope to regulation.

4. For the decision that defines the objectives of the in-depth review process, see Decision 2/CP.1 of the Conference of the Parties (1995). For a review of the experience, see document FCCC/CP/1998/4 at http://www.unfccc.de/resource/docs/cop4/04.pdf.

5. For more on the importance of the shared modeling activities in the European acid rain regime, see Levy (1993, 1995).

6. For more on the growing awareness among EU members and institutions that EU countries are not on track for compliance with the Kyoto targets, and for discussion of the emerging EU policy on how to reform Kyoto's "flexible mechanisms," see Kirwin (1999). See also EC (2000).

APPENDIX

THE CAUSES AND EFFECTS OF GLOBAL WARMING

1. On decarbonization of the energy system, see Nakićenović (1997).

2. Typically, the gross emissions and uptake of carbon in ecosystems are large, but it is the net effect that matters most for the atmosphere. Small errors in measuring the gross fluxes can lead to large errors in estimating the net. For discussion of the particular issues surrounding the measurement of carbon fluxes, see Watson et al. (2000). See also my discussion in chapter 3 of this book on the difficulties in measuring net fluxes of carbon related to forests.

3. For more on the impact of "greenhouse gases" on the energy balance of the planet, see the chapter of the IPCC report on this topic

173

(Schimel et al., 1996). On the problems with measuring these other gases, see chapter 3 of this book. For efforts to include the non-CO_2 gases in models that can be used to project future emissions see, especially, Reilly et al. (1999) and Hansen et al. (2000). My focus here is on greenhouse gases, but I am mindful that some human activities, such as emission of sulfate aerosols (mainly the by-product of burning sulfur-containing coal) have an opposite effect and reduce temperature, although on average worldwide the net effect of human activities is towards warming.

4. For the most recent scenarios, developed for the Intergovernmental Panel on Climate Change (IPCC), and discussion of the factors that influence those scenarios, see Nakićenović et al. (2000).

5. The historical temperature record back to the late nineteenth century, when the large-scale burning of fossil fuels began, is compiled from measurements on land and from stations and ships in the ocean. However, it is vulnerable to flaws. Changes in the methods for measuring temperature make it hard to integrate one data set with another. Poor coverage, especially in the southern hemisphere and in the oceans, make the data set vulnerable to weighting where measurements are more numerous. The "heat island" effect, by which economic activity raises local temperatures, introduces upward bias especially in measurements near urban areas. There have been many efforts to account for these flaws. The ideal measurement program is systematic and from satellite, but that record is much shorter (less than three decades). To complicate matters further, the satellite and ground-based temperature records do not correspond perfectly and there has been an intense effort to explain that discrepancy. The issues are discussed in the IPCC report (Watson et al.,1996) and the latest information, notably on the discrepancy between satellite and ground-based measurements, will be a central topic in the new IPCC report (available 2001).

6. The best review of the efforts to spot the human "fingerprint" and of the current confidence in models for projecting future climates is in the reports of the Intergovernmental Panel on Climate Change (IPCC), Working Group 1 (Houghton et al., 1996). A new IPCC report is due out in 2001 and is likely to strengthen the conclusions from the 1996 report that the "fingerprint" has been spotted; it may also conclude that emissions of greenhouse gases could cause even larger increases in temperature over the next century than was previously thought. The best

brief, accessible and nontechnical review is by Wigley (1999). For a recent survey of uncertainties in the models that are used to project future climates, see Allen et al. (2000).

7. For an introduction to how to think about adaptation and the impacts of climate change, see, especially, Schelling (1983).

8. For more on the effects, the best comprehensive source is the IPCC report, Working Group 2 (Watson et al., 1996, part II). For more on relative risks in the industrialized and developing countries, see Kates et al. (1985). For an accessible analysis of the consequences of adaptation as well as climate change on coastal zones in the United States see Yohe et al. (2000); for a similarly accessible treatment of the impacts on agriculture see Mendelsohn (1999). A recently completed assessment suggests that the impacts on the United States will be larger (http://www.nacc.usgcrp.gov/); however, that assessment has been extremely controversial, in part because of disputes over whether it adequately accounted for the capacity to adapt to climate changes. Other countries have also conducted national assessments, and these can be reached through the "national information" pages of the Climate Change Secretariat's web site (http://www.unfccc.int). I have barely scratched the surface here and apologize to the authors of the hundreds of recent impact studies that I do not cite and for not mentioning the numerous other factors—beyond the capacity for adaptation—that also affect results from these studies. Policy choices require balancing the cost of controlling emissions and the benefits of less severe changes in climate; such an approach suggests the need for economic analysis. For an accessible overview of the issues in economic analysis and introduction to the main results of such analysis, see Weyant (2000). The most important economic model is the "DICE" model originally developed by Nordhaus; for a presentation of the most recent version of that model, see Nordhaus and Boyer (2000).

9. A study by Broecker (1987) first called attention to this issue. Some work has been done to quantify the risks (e.g., Stocker and Schmittner, 1998).

10. For an example, see Still et al. (1999).

11. For a study that explores the implications of catastrophic change on the "optimal" strategy for slowing global warming, see, e.g., Keller et al. (2000).

AFTERWORD

1. See Victor (2001).

2. The actual deal on the enforcement mechanism was a lot more complex and included special language that allowed Japan to claim to itself that the consequences of noncompliance were not binding, which in turn made it easier for Japan to ward off industrialists at home who feared that Kyoto would be too costly to implement. COP-6bis also reached agreement on the rules for the Clean Development Mechanism (CDM) and emission trading and tied up most other loose ends. The deal itself was largely formalized at a meeting that fall in Marrakesh, known as COP-7. As a legal matter, the deal would not formally enter into force until Kyoto itself entered into force. At that time, the first meeting of the parties to the Kyoto Protocol (the so-called MOP-1) would take place, and these parties would formally adopt the cluster of decisions that had been forwarded to them by COP-7.

3. Victor (2002).

4. See Kagan (2002).

5. Note to auditors: I am mindful that it is illegal to fly a foreign carrier on U.S. government business when a flight on a U.S. airline is available. The workaround for this problem is code sharing—a ticket issued by Delta Airlines but flown with French pilots and equipment. In this era of efficient globalization, the U.S. government's inspiration in procurement remains unabashedly mercantilist.

6. McKibben and Wilcoxen (2003). For years, Resources for the Future has advanced this idea of a safety valve. See Kopp (1999). For an admirably sustained political effort to advance this idea, see also the Climate Policy Center (formerly "Americans for Equitable Climate Solutions") at http://www.cpc-inc.org/.

7. The European system has a safety valve built into it as well, though its architects don't use the same language. By controlling the barrier around the European system, in effect the EU is able to regulate the influx of inexpensive permits and thus regulate the cost of compliance inside the European zone. One can be sure that if prices inside the EU spike too high—beyond what European industry, ever sensitive to their international competitiveness can bear—the external spigot probably will be opened, putting in effect a cap on prices.

8. See, for example, the PCF's flagship projects in Brazil ("Plantar") and Chile ("Chacabuquito"), which detail the methods for calculating emission credits that could be offered through the CDM over the projects' twenty-one-year lifetimes. They require hypothetical estimations of power plant dispatch rules (for Chacabuquito) and expectations about the behavior of the U.S. steel market (for Plantar) that are difficult to defend. For more, see project documentation at http://prototype carbonfund.org.

9. Heller and Shukla (2003).

Works Cited

Abbott, Kenneth W., and Duncan Snidal. 2000. Hard and soft law in international governance. *International Organization* 54: 421–456.

Abbott, Kenneth W., Robert O. Keohane, Andrew Moravcsik, Anne-Marie Slaughter, and Duncan Snidal. 2000. The concept of legalization. *International Organization* 54: 401–419.

Albright, M. 1998. Earth Day 1998: Global problems and global solutions. Speech at the National Museum of Natural History, Washington, D.C., 21 April.

Allen, Marlon B. 1999. Researchers urge use of tradable permits for industry, CO_2 tax for other sectors. *International Environment Reporter* 22 (29 September): 795–796.

Allen, Myles R., Peter A. Stott, John F. B. Mitchell, Reiner Schnur, and Thomas L. Delworth. 2000. Quantifying the uncertainty in forecasts of anthropogenic climate change, *Nature* 401: 617–620.

Ausubel, J. H. 1991. Does climate still matter? *Nature* 350: 649–653.

Ausubel, J.H., and D. G. Victor. 1992. Verification of international environmental agreements. *Annual Review of Energy and Environment* 17: 1–43.

Barrett, S. 1998. Political economy of the Kyoto Protocol. *Oxford Review of Economic Policy* 14: 20–39.

Baumert, Kevin A., Nancy Kete, and Christiana Figueres. 2000. Designing the clean development mechanism to meet the needs of a broad range of interests. *World Resources Institute Climate Notes.* August. Washington, D.C.: World Resources Institute. http://www.wri.org/cdm/pdf/cdm-note2.pdf.

Benedick, Richard E. 1998. *Ozone diplomacy: New directions in safeguarding the planet.* Cambridge, Mass.: Harvard University Press.

Beuermann, Christiane, Thomas Langrock, and Hermann E. Ott. 2000. *Evaluation of (non-sink) AIJ-projects in developing countries (Ensadec).* Wuppertal, Germany: Wuppertal Institute for Climate, Environment and Energy. www.wupperinst.org.

Birnie, P. W., and A. E. Boyle. 1992. *International law and the environment.* New York: Clarendon Press.

BP Amoco. 2000. *Statistical review of world energy.* London: BP Amoco. http://bp.com/worldenergy.

Brack, Duncan. 1996. *International trade and the Montreal Protocol.* London: Royal Institute of International Affairs.

Broecker, Wallace S. 1987. Unpleasant surprises in the greenhouse. *Nature* 328: 123.

Brown Weiss, E., and H. K. Jacobson, eds. 1998. *Engaging countries: Strengthening compliance with international accords.* Cambridge, Mass.: MIT Press.

Bull, H. 1977. *The anarchical society: A study of order in world politics.* New York: Columbia University Press.

Byrd, R. C. and C. Hagel. 1998. Advice to heed on the Kyoto treaty. *Washington Post,* 6 May, p. A19.

Cai, Z. C., H. Tsuruta, and K. Minami. 2000. Methane emission from rice fields in China: Measurements and influencing factors. *Journal of Geophysical Research* 105: 17231–17242.

Cannell, M. G. R., R. Milne, K. J. Hargreaves, T. A. W. Brown, M. M. Cruickshank, R. I. Bradley, T. Spencer, D. Hope, M. F. Billett, W. N. Adger, and S. Subak. 1999. National inventories of terrestrial carbon sources and sinks: The U.K. experience. *Climatic Change* 42: 505–530.

Charnovitz, S. 1994. Encouraging environmental cooperation through the Pelly amendment. *Journal of Environment and Development* 3: 3–28.

————. 1998. Environment and health under WTO dispute settlement. *The International Lawyer* 32: 901–921.

Chayes, A., and A. H. Chayes. 1995. *The new sovereignty: Compliance with international regulatory agreements.* Cambridge, Mass.: Harvard University Press.

Climate Change Secretariat. 1999. Amendment to Annex I to the convention: Proposal from the Republic of Kazakhstan to amend the convention. Conference of the parties to the Framework Convention on Climate Change, fifth session. Bonn, Germany: Climate Change Secretariat. http://www.unfccc.int/resource/docs/cop5/02.pdf.

Clinton Administration. 1998. The Kyoto Protocol and the President's policies to address climate change: Administration economic analysis. July. Council of Economic Advisers.

Coase, Ronald H. 1960. The problem of social cost. *Journal of Law and Economics* 3: 1–44.

Cohen, Linda R., and Roger G. Noll. 1991. *The technology pork barrel.* Washington, D.C.: The Brookings Institution.

Conference of the Parties. 1995. Report of the conference of the parties on its first session, FCCC/CP/1995/7 and FCCC/CP/1995/7/Add.1. Bonn, Germany: Climate Change Secretariat. www.unfccc.de.

————. 1996. Report of the conference of the parties on its second session, FCCC/CP/1996/15 and FCCC/CP/1996/15/Add.1. Bonn, Germany: Climate Change Secretariat. www.unfccc.de.

————. 1997. Report of the conference of the parties on its third session, FCCC/CP/1997/7 and FCCC/CP/1997/7/Add.1. Bonn, Germany: Climate Change Secretariat. www.unfccc.de.

————. 1998. Report of the conference of the parties on its fourth session, FCCC/CP/1998/16 and FCCC/CP/1998/16/Add.1. Bonn, Germany: Climate Change Secretariat. www.unfccc.de.

Cook, E. 1995. *Lifetime commitments: Why climate policy-makers can't afford to overlook fully fluorinated compounds.* Washington, D.C.: World Resources Institute.

Cooper, R. N. 1998. Toward a real treaty on global warming. *Foreign Affairs* 77 (2): 66–79.

————. 1999. International approaches to global climate change. Paper 99-03. Cambridge, Mass.: Weatherhead Center for International Affairs, Harvard University.

Council on Environmental Quality (CEQ). 1997. *Environmental quality: The annual report of the Council on Environmental Quality.* Washington, D.C.: Government Printing Office.

Dales, J. H. 1968. *Pollution, property and prices: An essay in policymaking and economics.* Toronto: University of Toronto Press.

Department of Justice. 1990. A "comprehensive" approach to addressing potential global climate change. Discussion paper presented at an informal State Department seminar, 3 February).

Dixit, Avinash K. 1996. *The making of economic policy: A transaction-cost politics perspective.* Cambridge, Mass.: MIT Press.

Dooley, J. J. 1998. Unintended consequences: Energy R&D in a deregulated energy market. *Energy Policy* 26: 547.

Downing, P. B., and G. L. Brady. 1981. The role of citizen interest groups in environmental policy formation. Pages 61–93 in *Nonprofit firms in a three sector economy,* edited by M. White. Washington, D.C.: Urban Institute.

Downs, G. W., D. M. Rocke, and P. Barsoom. 1996. Is the good news about compliance good news about cooperation? *International Organization* 50: 379–406.

———. 1998. Managing the evolution of multilateralism. *International Organization* 52: 397–419.

Dudek, D. J., and J. B. Wiener. 1996. Joint implementation, transaction costs, and climate change. OECD/GD(96)173. Paris: Organization for Economic Cooperation and Development.

Eizenstat, S. E. and F. E. Loy. 1998. Hot air on climate change. *Washington Post,* 7 December, p. A25.

Energy Information Administration (EIA). 1999. Emission of carbon from energy sources in the United States: 1988 flash estimate. June. Washington, D.C.: Energy Information Administration. http://www.eia.doe.gov/oiaf/1605/flash/flash.html.

Environmental Protection Agency (EPA). Methane and Utilities Branch. 1998. *Cost of reducing methane emissions in the United States.* Washington, D.C.: Environmental Protection Agency.

———. Office of Policy. 2000. *Inventory of U.S. greenhouse gas emissions and sinks: 1990–1998.* Draft report, EPA 236-R-00–001. Washington, D.C.: Environmental Protection Agency.

Epstein, Joshua M., and Raj Gupta. 1990. *Controlling the greenhouse effect: Five global regimes compared*. Brookings Occasional Papers. Washington, D.C.: The Brookings Institution.

European Commission (EC). 2000. Green paper on greenhouse gas emissions trading within the European Union. COM(2000)87, 8 March. Brussels: European Commission. http://europa.eu.int/comm/environment/docum/0087_en.pdf.

Farer, T. J., and F. Gaer. 1993. The U.N. and human rights: At the end of the beginning. Chap. 8 in *United nations, divided world: The UN's roles in international relations*, edited by A. Roberts and B. Kingsbury. Oxford: Clarendon Press.

Flavin, Christopher. 1999. World carbon emissions fall. Worldwatch News Brief, 27 July. http://www.worldwatch.org/alerts/990727.html.

Foster, Vivien, and Robert W. Hahn. 1995. Designing more efficient markets: Lessons from Los Angeles smog control. *Journal of Law and Economics* 38: 19–48.

Franck, Thomas M. 1990. *The power of legitimacy among nations*. New York: Oxford University Press.

———. 1995. *Fairness in international law and institutions*. New York: Oxford University Press.

Gates, Paul W. 1968. *History of public land law development*. Report for the Public Land Law Review Commission. Washington, D.C.: Government Printing Office.

General Accounting Office (GAO). 1992. *International environment: International agreements are not well monitored*. GAO/RCED-92–43. Washington, D.C.: General Accounting Office.

Goldberg, D. M., S. Porter, N. LaCasta, and E. Hillman. 1998. Responsibility for non-compliance under the Kyoto Protocol's mechanisms for cooperative implementation. Washington, D.C.: Center for International Environmental Law and Lisbon: Euronatura.

Government of Brazil. 1997. Proposed elements of a protocol to the United Nations Framework Convention on Climate Change, presented by Brazil in response to the Berlin Mandate. FCCC/AGBM/1997/MISC.1/Add.3. Bonn, Germany: Climate Change Secretariat. www.unfccc.int.

Grubb, M. 1988. *The greenhouse effect: Negotiating targets*. London: Royal Institute of International Affairs.

Grubb, M., C. Vrolijk, and D. Brack. 1999. *The Kyoto Protocol: A guide and assessment.* London: Royal Institute of International Affairs.

Grübler, A., N. Nakićenović, and D. G. Victor. 1999. Dynamics of energy technologies and global change. *Energy Policy* 27: 247–280.

Gummer, John, and Robert Moreland. 2000. *The European Union & global climate change: A review of five national programmes.* Washington, D.C.: Pew Center on Global Climate Change.

Hahn, R. W. 1998. *The economics and politics of climate change.* AEI Studies on Global Environmental Policy. Washington, D.C.: American Enterprise Institute.

Hahn, R. W., and G. L. Hester. 1989. Where did all the markets go? An analysis of EPA's Emission Trading Program." *Yale Journal on Regulation* 6: 109–153.

Hahn, R. W., and R. N. Stavins. 1999. *What has Kyoto wrought? The real architecture of international tradeable permit markets.* Washington, D.C.: American Enterprise Institute.

Hamilton, Clive, and Lins Vellen. 1999. Land-use change in Australia and the Kyoto Protocol. *Environmental Science and Policy* 2: 145–152.

Hansen, James, Makiko Sato, Reto Ruedy, Andrew Lacis, and Valdar Oinas. 2000. Global warming in the twenty-first century: An alternative scenario. *Proceedings of the National Academy of Sciences* 97: 9875–9880.

Hart, Oliver. 1995. *Firms, contracts, and financial structure.* Oxford: Clarendon Press.

Hayhoe, K., A. Jain, H. Pitcher, C. MacCracken, M. Gibbs, D. Wuebbles, R. Harvey, and D. Kruger. 1999. Costs of multigreenhouse gas reduction targets for the USA. *Science* 286: 905–906.

Heinz Center. 1999. *Technology policies for reducing greenhouse gas emissions: A project summary.* Washington, D.C.: H. John Heinz Center for Science, Economics and the Environment.

Heller, Thomas C., and P. R. Shukla. 2003. Development and climate: Engaging developing countries. Pages 111–40 in *Beyond Kyoto: Advancing the international effort against climate change.* Washington, D.C.: Pew Center on Global Climate Change. http://www.pew climate.org/docUploads/Development%20and%20Climate%Epdf.

Henkin, L. 1979. *How nations behave: Law and foreign policy,* 2nd ed. New York: Columbia University Press.

Hogue, C. 1998. Countries set deadline for elaborating rules on trading, emission offset projects abroad. *International Environment Reporter* 21 (25 November): 1151–1152.

Houghton, J. J., L. G. Meiro Filho, B. A. Callander, N. Harris, A. Kattenberg, and K. Maskell, eds. 1996. *Climate change 1995—The science of climate change.* Contribution of Working Group I to the Second Assessment Report of the Intergovernmental Panel on Climate Change. Cambridge, Mass.: Cambridge University Press.

Hufbauer, G. C., J. J. Schott, and K. A. Elliott. 1990. *Economic sanctions reconsidered,* 2nd ed. Washington, D.C.: Institute for International Economics.

International Environment Reporter. 1996. Conservation information submitted to EEA incomplete; lack of national inventories, low priority of data collection cited. *International Environment Reporter* 19 (30 October): 992–997.

———. 1998. Liability for emission trades should rest with allowance sellers, RFF official says." *International Environment Reporter* 21 (14 October): 1019.

———. 2000. Commission adopts CO_2 reduction accords negotiated with Korean, Japanese carmakers. *International Environmental Reporter* 23 (26 April): 341.

Jacoby, Henry D., Ronald G. Prinn, and Richard Schmalensee. 1998. Kyoto's unfinished business. *Foreign Affairs* 77 (4, July/August): 54–67.

Jonas, M., S. Nilsson, M. Obersteiner, M. Gluck, and Y. Ermoliev. 1999. Verification times underlying the Kyoto Protocol: Global benchmark calculations. Interim Report, 99-062. Laxenburg, Austria: International Institute for Applied Systems Analysis.

Joskow, Paul L., and Richard Schmalensee. 1998. The political economy of market-based environmental policy: The U.S. acid rain program. *Journal of Law and Economics* 41: 37–83.

Joskow, Paul L., R. Schmalensee, and E. M. Bailey. 1998. The market for sulfur dioxide emission. *The American Economic Review* 88:669–685.

Kagan, Robert. 2002. *Of paradise and power: America and Europe in the new world order.* New York: Knopf.

Kates, Robert W., Jesse H. Ausubel, and Mimi Berberian, eds. 1985. *Climate impact assessment: Studies of the interaction of climate and society.* Published for the Scientific Committee on Problems of the Environment of the International Council of Scientific Unions. New York: Wiley & Sons.

Keesing, D. B. 1998. *Improving trade policy reviews in the World Trade Organization.* Washington, D.C: Institute for International Economics.

Keith, David W., and Hadi Dowlatabadi. 1992. Taking geoengineering seriously. *Eos, Transactions, American Geophysical Union* 73: 289–293.

Keller, Klaus, Kelvin Tan, François M. M. Morel, and David F. Bradford. 2000. Preserving the ocean circulation: Implications for climate policy, *Climatic Change* 47: 17–43.

Keohane, Robert O. 1989. *International institutions and state power: Essays in international relations theory.* Boulder, Colo.: Westview Press.

Kerr, Suzi. 1998. Enforcing compliance: The allocation of liability in international GHG emissions trading and the clean development mechanism. Issue Brief N. 15, October. Washington, D.C.: Resources for the Future.

Kirwin, Joe. 1999. EU greenhouse gas emissions rising; commission seeks action on "alarming" trend." *International Environment Reporter* 22 (11): 433–434.

Kopp, Raymond. 1999. Definitions of Kyoto compliance: Reducing uncertainty and enhancing prospects for ratification. November. Washington, D.C.: Resources for the Future.

Krasner, Stephen D., ed., 1983. *International regimes.* Ithaca, N.Y.: Cornell University Press.

Lanchbery, J. 1998. Long-term trends in systems for implementation review in international agreements on fauna and flora. Chap. 2 in *The implementation and effectiveness of international environmental commitments: Theory and practice,* edited by D. G. Victor, K. Raustiala, and E. B. Skolnikoff. Cambridge, Mass.: MIT Press.

Lempert, Robert J., and Michael Schlesinger. 2000. Robust strategies for abating climate change. *Climatic Change* 45: 387–401.

Leonard, H. Jeffrey. 1988. *Pollution and the struggle for the world product: Multinational corporations, environment, and international comparative advantage.* Cambridge, Mass.: Cambridge University Press.

Levy, M. A. 1993. European acid rain: The power of tote-board diplomacy. Chap. 3 in *Institutions for the earth: Sources of effective international environmental protection,* edited by P. M. Haas, R. O. Keohane, and M. A. Levy. Cambridge, Mass.: MIT Press.

————. 1995. International cooperation to combat acid rain. In *Green Globe Yearbook, 1995*, edited by Helge Ole Bergesen and Georg Parmann. Oxford: Oxford University Press.

Lile, R., M. Powell, and M. Toman. 1998. Implementing the clean development mechanism: Lessons from U.S. private-sector participation in activities implemented jointly. Discussion Paper 99-08. Washington, D.C.: Resources for the Future.

Liski, J., T. Karjalainen, A. Pussinen, G.-J. Nabuurs, and P. Kauppi. 2000. Trees as carbon sinks and sources in the European Union. *Environmental Science and Policy* 3: 91–97.

Low, Patrick, ed. 1992. *International trade and the environment*. World Bank Discussion Papers No. 159. Washington, D.C.: World Bank.

MacCracken, Christopher N., Jae A. Edmonds, Son H. Kim, and Ronald D. Sands. 1999. The economics of the Kyoto Protocol. *The Energy Journal*. (Kyoto Special Issue): 25–73.

Manne, Alan, and R. Richels. 1999. The Kyoto Protocol: A Cost-Effective Strategy for Meeting Environmental Objectives? *The Energy Journal*. (Kyoto Special Issue): 1–23.

Margolis, Robert M., and Daniel M. Kammen. 1999. Underinvestment: The energy technology and R&D policy challenge. *Science* 528: 690–692.

Marland, G., R. J. Andres, and T. A. Boden. 1993. Carbon dioxide emissions. In *Trends '93, A compendium of data on global change*. Oak Ridge, Tenn.: Carbon Dioxide Information Analysis Center, Oak Ridge National Laboratory.

Martin, L. L. 1992. *Coercive cooperation: Explaining multilateral economic sanctions*. Princeton, N.J.: Princeton University Press.

McKibbin, W. J., and P. J. Wilcoxen. 1997. A better way to slow global climate change. Brookings Policy Brief No. 17. Washington, D.C.: Brookings Institution.

————. 2003. *Climate change policy after Kyoto: Blueprint for a realistic approach*. Washington, D.C.: Brookings Institution.

Mendelsohn, Robert. 1999. *The greening of global warming*. AEI Studies on Global Environmental Policy. Washington, DC: American Enterprise Institute.

Mitchell, R. 1994. Regime design matters: Intentional oil pollution and treaty compliance. *International Organization* 48: 425–458.

Moravcsik, A. 1997. Taking preferences seriously: A liberal theory of international politics. *International Organization* 51: 513–553.

Morgan, M. Granger, and Susan F. Tierney, 1998. Research support for the power industry. *Issues in Science and Technology* 15: 81–87.

Mosier, A. R., J. M. Duxbury, J. R. Freney, O. Heinemeyer, K. Minami, and D. E. Johnson. 1998. Mitigating agricultural emissions of methane. *Climatic Change* 40: 39–80.

Nakićenović, Nebojša. 1997. Freeing energy from carbon. In *Technological trajectories and the human environment*, edited by J. H. Ausubel and H. D. Langford. Washington, D.C.: National Academy Press.

Nakićenović, N., A. Grübler, and A. McDonald. 1998. *Global energy perspectives.* Cambridge: Cambridge University Press.

Nakićenović, Nebojša, Nadejda Victor, and T. Morita. 1999. Emissions scenario database and review of scenarios. *Mitigation and Adaptation Strategies for Global Change* 3: 95–120.

Nakićenović, N., O. Davidson, G. Davis, A. Grübler, T. Kram, E. La Rovere, B. Metz, T. Morita, W. Pepper, H. Pitcher, et al. 2000. *Emissions scenarios: An IPCC special report.* Cambridge: Cambridge University Press.

Neue, H. U., and J. Boonjawat, 1998. Methane emissions from rice fields. Chap. 8 in *Asian change in the context of global climate change: Impact of natural and anthropogenic changes in Asia on global biogeochemistry*, edited by J. Galloway and J. Melillo. Cambridge: Cambridge University Press.

Nilsson, Sten, Anatoly Shvidenko, Vladimiar Stolbovoi, Michael Gluck, Matthias Jonas, and Michael Obersteiner. 2000. Full carbon account for Russia. Interim Report, IR-00–021. Laxenburg, Austria: International Institute for Applied Systems Analysis. http://www.iiasa.ac.at./Admin/PUB/Documents/IR-00-021.pdf

Nordhaus, Robert R., Kyl W. Danish, Richard H. Rosenzweig, and Britt Speyer Fleming. 2000. A framework for achieving environmental integrity and the economic benefits of emissions trading under the Kyoto Protocol. *The Environmental Law Reporter* 30: 11061–11070.

Nordhaus, William D., and J. Boyer, 2000. *Warming the world: Economic models of global warming.* Cambridge, Mass.: MIT Press.

North, Douglass Cecil. 1990. *Institutions, institutional change, and economic performance.* Cambridge; New York: Cambridge University Press.

Olson, Mancur. 1965. *The logic of collective action: Public goods and the theory of groups.* Cambridge, Mass.: Harvard University Press.

Olson, M., and R. Zeckhauser, 1966. An economic theory of alliances. *Review of Economics and Statistics* 48: 266–279.

Ostrom, Elinor. 1990. *Governing the commons: The evolution of institutions for collective action.* Cambridge: Cambridge University Press.

Ostrom, Elinor, Joanna Burger, Christopher B. Field, Richard B. Norgaard, and David Policansky. 1999. Revisiting the commons: Local lessons, global challenges. *Science* 284: 278–282.

Oye, Kenneth A. 1986. Explaining cooperation under anarchy: Hypotheses and strategies. Chap. 1 in *Cooperation under anarchy*, edited by K. A. Oye. Princeton, N.J.: Princeton University Press.

Parson, Edward A. 1993. Protecting the ozone layer. Pages 27–73 in *Institutions for the earth: Sources of effective international environmental protection*, edited by Peter M. Haas, Robert O. Keohane, and Marc A. Levy. Cambridge, Mass.: MIT Press.

Parson, Edward A., and Owen J. Greene. 1995. Ozone since London: Recent progress and current issues in international protection of the ozone layer. *Environment* 37 (2): 16–20, and 35–43.

Pigou, A. C. [1920/1932] 1952. *The economics of welfare.* 4th ed. London: MacMillan.

Pinard, Michelle, and Francis Putz. 1997. Monitoring carbon sequestration benefits associated with a reduced-impact logging project in Malaysia. *Mitigation and Adaptation Strategies for Global Change* 2: 203–215.

Pizer, William A. 1999. Choosing prices or quantity controls for greenhouse gases. Climate Change Brief No. 17. Washington, D.C.: Resources for the Future.

President's Committee of Advisors on Science and Technology (PCAST). 1997. Federal energy research and development: Challenges for the twenty-first century. Panel on Energy Research and Development. November. Washington, D.C.: The White House.

———. 1999. The federal role in international cooperation on energy innovation. Panel on International Cooperation in Energy Research, Development and Deployment. June. Washington, D.C.: The White House.

Rabkin, J. 1998. *Why sovereignty matters.* AEI Studies on Global Environmental Policy. Washington, D.C.: American Enterprise Institute.

Raiffa, H. 1982. *The art and science of negotiation.* Cambridge, Mass.: Harvard University Press.

Raustiala, K., and D. G. Victor. 1998. Conclusions. Pages 659–707 in *The implementation and effectiveness of international environmental commitments: Theory and practice,* edited by D. G. Victor, K. Raustiala, and E. B. Skolnikoff. Cambridge, Mass.: MIT Press.

Reilly, J., R. Prinn, J. Harnisch, J. Fitzmaurice, H. Jacoby, D. Kicklighter, J. Melillo, P. Stone, A. Sokolov, and C. Wang. 1999. Multi-gas assessment of the Kyoto Protocol. *Nature* 401: 549–555.

Roberts, M. J., and M. Spence. 1976. Effluent charges and licenses under uncertainty. *Journal of Environmental Economics and Management* 5: 193–208.

Russell, C. S., W. Harrington, and W. J. Vaughan. 1986. *Enforcing pollution control laws.* Washington, D.C.: Resources for the Future.

Sand, P. H. 1997. Commodity or taboo? International regulation of trade in endangered species. Pages 19–36 in *Green Globe Yearbook 1995,* edited by H. O. Bergesen and G. Parmann. New York: Oxford University Press.

Schelling, T. C. 1960. *The strategy of conflict.* Cambridge, Mass.: Harvard University Press.

———. 1983. Climatic change: Implications for welfare and policy. In *Changing climate: Report of the carbon dioxide assessment committee.* Washington, D.C.: National Academy Press.

———. 1997. The cost of combating global warming. *Foreign Affairs* 76 (November/December): 8–14.

———. 1998. *Costs and benefits of greenhouse gas reduction.* AEI Studies on Global Environmental Policy. Washington, D.C.: American Enterprise Institute.

Schiffman, Howard S. 1999. The southern bluefin tuna case: ITLOS hears its first fishery dispute. *Journal of International Wildlife Law & Policy* 2: 318ff.

Schimel, David, et al. 1996. Radiative forcing of climate change. Pages 65–131 in *Climate change 1995: The science of climate change,* edited by J. T. Houghton, L. G. Meira Filh, B. A. Callander, N. Harris, A. Kattenberg, and K. Maskell. Cambridge: Cambridge University Press.

———. 2000. Contribution of increasing CO_2 and climate to carbon storage by ecosystems in the United States." *Science* 287: 2004–2006.

Schlamadinger, Bernard, and Gregg Marland. 2000. *Land use and global climate change: Forests, land management and the Kyoto Protocol.* Washington, D.C.: Pew Center on Global Climate Change.

Schlesinger, William H. 1999. Carbon sequestration in soils. *Science* 284: 2095.

Schmalensee, Richard. 1998. Greenhouse policy architectures and institutions. Pages 137–158 in *Economics and policy issues in climate change.* Edited by William D. Nordhaus. Washington, D.C.: Resources for the Future.

Schmalensee, Richard., P. L. Joskow, A. D. Ellerman, J. P. Montero, and E. M. Bailey. 1998. An interim evaluation of sulfur dioxide emissions trading. *Journal of Economic Perspectives* 12: 53–68.

Schneider, Stephen H., and Lawrence H. Goulder. 1997. Achieving low-cost emissions targets. *Nature* 389: 13–14.

Schwebel, Stephen M., Florentino Feliciano, Kenneth Keith, Per Tresselt, and Chusei Yamada. 2000. Southern bluefin tuna case: Australia and New Zealand v. Japan. Award on Jurisdiction and Admissibility, rendered by Arbitral Tribunal constituted under Annex VII of the United Nations Convention on the Law of the Sea, 4 August.

Sebenius, James K. 1983. Negotiation arithmetic: Adding and subtracting issues and parties. *International Organization* 37: 281–316.

Secretary of Energy Advisory Board (SEAB). 1995. Energy R&D: Shaping our nation's future in a competitive world. Final Report of the Task Force on Strategic Energy Research and Development. Washington, D.C.: Secretary of Energy Advisory Board.

Shogren, Jason. 1999. *The benefits and costs of the Kyoto Protocol.* AEI Studies on Global Environmental Policy. Washington, D.C.: American Enterprise Institute.

Shubik, Martin. 1982. *Game theory in the social sciences: Concepts and solutions* Cambridge, Mass.: MIT Press.

Shvidenko, A., and S. Nilsson. 1998. Phytomass, increment, mortality and carbon budget of Russian forests. Interim Report, IR-98–105. December. Laxenburg, Austria: International Institute for Applied Systems Analysis. http://www.iiasa.ac.at/Publications/Documents/IR-98-105.pdf.

Slaughter [Burley], A.-M. 1992. Toward an age of liberal nations. *Harvard International Law Journal* 33: 393–405.

Slaughter [Burley], A.-M. 1995. International law in a world of liberal states. *European Journal of International Law* 6 (4): 503–538.

Speer, L. J. 2000. France: Country finalizing climate change action plan that includes energy tax. *International Environment Reporter* 23: 49–50.

Stavins, R. N. 1998. What can we learn from the grand policy experiment? Lessons from SO_2 allowance trading. *Journal of Economic Perspectives* 12: 69–88.

Still, Christopher J., Prudence Foster, and Stephen H. Schneider, 1999. Simulating the effects of climate change on tropical montane cloud forests. *Nature* 398: 608–610.

Stocker, Thomas F., and Andreas Schmittner. 1998. Influence of CO_2 emission rates on the stability of the thermohaline circulation. *Nature* 388: 862–865.

Subak, S. 2000. Agricultural soil carbon accumulation in North America: Considerations for climate policy. Policy Papers. February. Washington, D.C.: Natural Resources Defense Council. http://www.nrdc.org/globalWarming/psoil.asp.

Tenner, Edward. 1996. *Why things bite back: Technology and the revenge of unintended consequences.* New York: Knopf.

United Nations Economic Commission for Europe and Food and Agriculture Organization of the United Nations (UNECE/FAO). 2000. Woody biomass and the carbon cycle. Chap. IIIb in *Forest Resources of Europe, CIS, North America, Australia, Japan and New Zealand (industrialized temperate/boreal countries).* UNECE/FAO contribution to *Global Forest Resources Assessment 2000.* New York: United Nations.

United States Environmental Protection Agency (USEPA). 2000. Inventory of U.S. greenhouse gas emissions and sinks: 1990–1998. EPA 236-R-00-001, draft for public comment. Washington, D.C.: Environmental Protection Agency.

United States Government. 2000. United States submission on land use, land-use change, and forestry. In Methodological issues: Land Use, land-use change and forestry. 1 August. United Nations Framework Convention on Climate Change, Subsidiary Body for Scientific and Technological Advice. Submissions from Parties. FCCC/SBSTA/2000/MISC.6/Add.1. *http://www.unfccc.de/resource/docs/2000/sbsta/misc06a01.pdf.*

United States Senate. 1997. S.R. 98, 105th Congress, 1st session. Report No. 105-54.

———. 1998. S.R. 86, 105th Congress, 2nd session. Report No. 105-170.

Victor, D. G. 1991a. How to slow global warming. *Nature* 349: 451–456.

———. 1991b. Limits of market-based strategies for slowing global warming: The case of tradeable permits. *Policy Sciences* 24: 199–222.

———. 1997. The use and effectiveness of nonbinding instruments in the management of complex international environmental problems. In *Proceedings of the American Society of International Law*, 91st Annual Meeting, pp. 241–250.

———. 1998a. The operation and effectiveness of the Montreal Protocol's non-compliance procedure. Chap. 4 in *The implementation and effectiveness of international environmental commitments: Theory and practice*, edited by D. G. Victor, K. Raustiala, and E. B. Skolnikoff. Cambridge, Mass.: MIT Press.

———. 1998b. The regulation of greenhouse gases—does fairness matter? Chap. 12 in *Fair weather? Equity concerns in climate change*, edited by F. Tóth. London: Earthscan.

———. 1998c. Kyoto shell game. *Washington Post*, 20 November, P. A29.

———. 1999. On the economics and politics of early action to slow global warming. 26 May. Council on Foreign Relations, New York. Mimeographed.

———. 2000. The trading world can do without a "millennium round." *International Herald Tribune*, 26 January, op-ed page.

———. 2001. Piety at Kyoto didn't cool the planet. *New York Times*, 23 March, p. A19 (op-ed).

———. 2002. Weak on warming. *Washington Post*. 19 February, p. A15.

Victor, D. G., and J. Salt. 1995. Keeping the climate treaty relevant. *Nature* 373: 280–282.

Victor, D. G., and G. J. MacDonald. 1999. Future emissions of long-lived potent greenhouse gases: Sulfur hexafluoride and perfluorocarbons. *Climatic Change* 42: 633–662.

Victor, D. G., and E. B. Skolnikoff. 1999. Translating intent into action: Implementing environmental commitments. *Environment* 41 (2 March): 16–20, and 39–44.

Victor, D. G., N. Nakićenović, and N. Victor. 2000. The Kyoto Protocol emission allocations: Windfall surpluses for Russia and Ukraine. *Climatic Change* (in press).

Victor, D. G., K. Raustiala, and E. B. Skolnikoff, eds. 1998. *The implementation and effectiveness of international environmental commitments: Theory and practice.* Cambridge, Mass.: MIT Press.

Vogel, David. 1995. *Trading up: Consumer and environmental regulation in a global economy.* Cambridge, Mass.: Harvard University Press.

Watson, Robert T., Marufu C. Zinyowera, and Richard H. Moss, eds. 1996. *Climate change 1995—Impacts, adaptations and mitigation of climate change: Scientific-technical analysis.* Contribution of Working Group II to the Second Assessment Report of the Intergovernmental Panel on Climate Change. Cambridge: Cambridge University Press.

Watson, R. T., I. R. Noble, B. Bolin, N. H. Ravindranath, D. J. Verardo, and D. J. Dokken, eds. 2000. *Land use, land-use change, and forestry: A special report of the IPCC.* Cambridge: Cambridge University Press.

Weitzman, M. L. 1974. Prices vs. quantities. *Review of Economic Studies* 41: 477–491.

Weyant, John P. 2000. *An introduction to the economics of climate change policy.* Arlington, Va.: Pew Center on Global Climate Change. www.pewclimate.org.

Wiener, Jonathan B. 1999. Global environmental regulation: Instrument choice in legal context. *The Yale Law Journal* 108: 677–800.

Wigley, Tom M. L. 1999. The science of climate change: Global and U.S. perspectives. Washington, D.C.: Pew Center on Global Climate Change.

Wigley, T. M. L., R. Richels, and J. A. Edmonds. 1996. Economic and environmental choices in the stabilization of atmospheric CO_2 concentrations. *Nature* 379: 240–243.

Wildavsky, A. 1980. Richer is safer. *Public Interest* 60 (summer): 23.

Wiser, Glenn M. 1999. *Compliance systems under multilateral agreements: A survey for the benefit of Kyoto Protocol policy makers.* Discussion draft. Washington, D.C.: Center for International Environmental Law.

Wood, R. A., A. B. Keen, J. F. B. Mitchell, and J. M. Gregory. 1999. Changing spatial structure of the thermohaline circulation in re-

194

sponse to atmospheric CO_2 forcing in a climate model. *Nature* 399: 572–575.

World Bank. 2000. *Greening industry: New roles for communities, markets, and governments.* New York: Oxford University Press.

World Trade Organization (WTO) Appellate Body. 1998. *United States—Import prohibition of certain shrimp and shrimp products,* WT/DS58/AB/R (12 October); reprinted in *International Legal Materials* 38 (1999): 121–175.

Yamin, F., and J. Lefevere. 2000. Designing options for implementing an emissions trading regime for greenhouse gases in the EC. 22 February. London: Foundation for International Environmental Law and Development.http://www.field.org.uk/fieldmain/PDF/ecet.pdf

Yohe, Gary, et al. 2000. *Sea-level rise and global climate change: A review of impacts to U.S. coasts.* Washington, D.C.: Pew Center on Global Climate Change. http://www.pewclimate.org/projects/env_sealevel.cfm.

Young, O. R. 1989a. The politics of international regime formation: Managing natural resources and the environment. *International Organization* 43: 349–375.

———. 1989b. *International cooperation: Building regimes for natural resources and the environment.* Ithaca, N.Y.: Cornell University Press.

Index

adaptation to climate change policies, 22, 120

Albright, Madeleine, 34

allocation of emission permits: as compensation, 37–39, 40–41; domestic and international systems compared, 45–50; expanding to developing countries, 33–36, 40–41; under a hybrid system, 20, 102–5; under the Kyoto Protocol, 26–29; participation strategy, problems of, 41–45; problems of, 11–14, 25–26, 29–33, 50–54; project-by-project credits, 36 (*see also* Clean Development Mechanism); as rewards, 39–41

architecture for greenhouse gas regulation. *See* greenhouse gas regulatory regime

Argentina, 34–36

"Assigned amounts." *See* emission permits

auctions: of emission permits, 46, 50–51; of mobile phone licenses in Europe, ix, 51

Australia, 63

banking of emission permits, 48–49

base years, 29

benchmarks, 95

Berlin Mandate, 14–15

borrowing of emission permits, 48–49

Brady plan, 71

"broad then deep" participation strategy, 41–45

BTU tax, 84

buyer liability, 21, 69, 71–74, 106

Byrd, Robert, 46

"cap and trade" system. *See* emission trading; Kyoto Protocol

carbon dioxide: annual emissions, 31–32; decarbonization, 99–100;

system); goal setting, undermining of, 23; greenhouse gases, lumping together of, 23–24; as greenhouse gas regulatory regime, 80; liberal zone of law enforcement, difficulty of implementing, 68; monitoring and the need to restrict targets, 75; need to reopen, 110–11; negotiating the, 7, 26, 29, 90–91; noncompliance procedures, 65; options for pursuing, 7–11; ratification of, viii–ix, 3; reluctance to reopen, 10–11, 18; sources and sinks of gases regulated by, 58

land use, and carbon dioxide flux, 60–61
leakage problem, 42–43, 85–86
liability rules. *See* compliance; enforcement
Loy, Frank, 34

Marshall Plan, 92, 95–96
MDIs. *See* metered-dose inhalers
metered-dose inhalers (MDIs), 16
methane, 23, 59–62, 118
MLF. *See* Multilateral Fund
mobile phone auctions (Europe), ix, 51
monitoring: carbon dioxide fluxes, problems posed by, 59–62; carbon taxes, 86–89; data, need for improved, 112–14; data, sources of, 56–57; under a hybrid system, 21, 105–6; incentives for improving, 111; multigas approach, problems of, 57–60, 62–63, 75; oil tankers, 60; policies and measures approach, 94; problems of, 17, 73
Montreal Protocol on Substances that Deplete the Ozone Layer (1987),

14–17; escape clause for essential uses, x–xi, 16–17, 21; monitoring under, 57; noncompliance procedures, 64–65; regulation of CFCs and HCFCs, 118; success and lessons of, x–xi
Multilateral Fund (MLF), 37

NGOs. *See* nongovernmental organizations
nitrous oxide, 60–61, 118
nongovernmental organizations (NGOs): enforcement, role in, 66–67; monitoring activities, 56–57

OECD. *See* Organization for Economic Cooperation and Development
oil tankers, monitoring, 60
Organization for Economic Cooperation and Development (OECD): Environmental Performance Reviews, 95; members of and the Kyoto Protocol, 32; mutual peer review procedures, 92
ozone depletion: Montreal Protocol, 14–16; Multilateral Fund, 37

participation strategies: broad then deep, 41–45; deep then broad, 44–45; under a hybrid system, 104–5
perfluorocarbons, 23, 58, 118
pledge and review proposal, 91
policies and measures approach: advantages of, 90–94; as greenhouse gas regulatory regime, 80; problems of, 94–96
policy options for greenhouse gas regulation. *See* greenhouse gas regulatory regime

"prices vs. quantities" debate, xii,
81–83
property rights: allocation of emission permits, problem of, 12;
emission permits as "assigned
amounts," 28; international law,
difficulty of securing under, xii,
13; need to allocate under Kyoto
Protocol, 76; permits under a
hybrid system, 104

Rabkin, J., 112
ratification, 3
research, need for government investment in, 21–22
Russia: banking of permits and,
49; emission credits windfall,
9–10, 13, 30, 32; emission credits
windfall, addressing problem of,
110, 113; emission credits windfall, impact of capping trading,
115; emission credits windfall,
political problems of, 104; forests
and carbon dioxide flux, 61;
global warming, expected benefits
of, 38

Schelling, Thomas, 77, 92
science, need for government investment in, 21–22
seller liability, 18, 69–73
sinks, carbon, 8–9, 59
sulfur hexafluoride, 23, 118
sulfur trading system, ix, 46, 57,
102

targets and timetables approach. See
emission trading system; Kyoto
Protocol
taxation: greenhouse gas taxes, 19,
79–89, 94; threat of and sulfur trading in the United States, 46

technology, need for government
investment in, 21–22
timetables, stretching out to ease
compliance, 11, 51–52
Toronto conference, 14, 90
trade, international: and a coordinated tax system, 83, 87–89;
emission limits and the leakage
problem, 42–43; enforcement of
agreements, 47–48
trading approach. See Kyoto
Protocol
treaties, requirement for universal
consent, 46–47

Ukraine: banking of permits and, 49;
emission credits windfall, 9–10,
13, 30, 32; emission credits windfall, addressing problem of, 110,
113; emission credits windfall,
impact of capping trading, 115;
emission credits windfall, political
problems of, 104
UNFCCC. See United Nations Framework Convention on Climate
Change
United Kingdom, 5
United Nations, as monitoring
agency, 62
United Nations Framework Convention on Climate Change
(UNFCCC), 44
United States: agriculture and carbon
sinks, 8; carbon dioxide emissions,
6, 13; compliance, requirements
for, 3–4; developing countries,
opposition to exemption of, 34,
37, 41; emission trading and the
cost of compliance, 5; enforcement of wildlife protection rules,
65; forests and carbon dioxide flux,
61; new thinking, need for, 115;